CW00410710

SPAGHETTI BOWL

Irishtown Press

SPAGHETTI BOWL

Cónal Creedon

Irishtown Press

Published in 2024 by Irishtown Press

irishtownpress@gmail.com

© Cónal Creedon 2024

The moral right of the author has been asserted.

A catalogue record for this book is available from the British Library.

ISBN 978-1-0687322-0-1 (hardcover)

ISBN 978-1-0687322-1-8 (paperback)

ISBN 978-1-0687322-2-5 (e-book)

All rights reserved. No part of this publication may be reproduced or transmitted in any form or by any means, electronic or mechanical, including photography, recording, or any information storage or retrieval system, without permission in writing from the publisher. The book is sold subject to the condition that it shall not, by way of trade or otherwise, be lent, resold or otherwise circulated without the publisher's prior consent in any form of binding or cover other than that in which it is published and without a similar condition, including this condition, being imposed on the subsequent purchaser.

IP-SB-K

To Fiona with love:
calm in the eye of the storm,
fearless in the face of adversity,
fun when laughs are thin on the ground,
continues to dance long after the band has packed up and gone home.

It takes a city to bring a manuscript from page to a bookshop shelf.

I am very grateful to John Foley and Lisa Sheridan of Bite Design for their ongoing support and encouragement. There are many others who deserve special mention, including Dominic Carroll for his editorial eye and guidance, and Arnoldzike Stankaityte for her enthusiasm, friendship and photography – and those who always seem to be in my corner reaching out the hand of friendship: Paul Moynihan, Mary McCarthy, Michelle Whelan, Donal O'Keeffe, Aisling Meath, Neil Prendeville, John Spillane, Liam Ronayne, Patricia Looney, Danny Morrison, Victoria Pearson, Helen Boyle, Ken Corr and Shirley Feehely.

I would like to take this opportunity to express my appreciation to the organisations across the city who continue to fly the flag for writers and readers: the School of English and Digital Humanities at UCC, Cork City Council, Cork City Libraries, the Crawford Art Gallery and the Munster Literature Centre. And of course, my gratitude to those on the front line: John Breen and all at Waterstone's bookshop in Cork.

I am blessed with so many friends, family and neighbours who continue to offer me unconditional encouragement – far too many to mention here by name.

Contents

Cónal with Finbarr on Devonshire Street. Photo: Michael MacSweeney.

Before I Begin

I sometimes wonder if the past and future are part of a time equilibrium paradox. Two fictional worlds precariously balanced on either side of the scales of myth and lore. The future speculates on what might be, while the past wallows in what might have been. The truth only exists in that very narrow band in the present – where both realities intersect.

Our relationship with the past can be complicated and sometimes contradictory. I recoil from nostalgia, yet am fascinated and irresistibly drawn to living tradition. And there is a difference: nostalgia is a highly curated museum piece on display, intact and preserved, while living tradition is subject to influence and change from all sides – and continues to boldly plough its own, often unpopular, evolutionary furrow. And though I respect the past, I am tantalised by the future and the ad hoc nature of anticipating the next chapter.

I'm inclined to believe that memoir, for the most part, is pure fiction – while fiction often presents as truth. That said, my work has inadvertently delved into the past on a number of occasions; in one way or another the film documentaries I've made have all been inspired by the spaghetti bowl of streets where I live, here in downtown Cork city. *The Immortal Deed of Michael O'Leary VC* (Cork City Library, 2014) deconstructs detailed aspects of my early childhood, while *Art Imitating Life Imitating Death* (Florence University Press, 2021; Irishtown Press, 2023) digs deep into the underbelly of this boy's creative process during a complicated time of life.

And so, to this collection.

Spaghetti Bowl is an anthology of previously published essays. For the most part they were commissioned as a commentary on some aspect of the present. Of course, the present for which they were originally published is now past. So, like time capsules, they stand testament to moments of another era. I found the articles written during the Covid pandemic to be particularly thought-provoking and reflect on a time which is barely recognisable. While the essay inspired by Eurovision was written during the Russian incursion into Ukraine – which seemed to unite and polarise the East and the West in equal measures – I could not have anticipated the far more divisive crisis that was to erupt in Palestine the following year.

In the course of compiling these essays, I found myself reading the anthology as a collection. And though the inspiration for each individual piece is very much a stand-alone exploration, the unifying dynamic in this compendium is the shared perspective of the world as viewed from my neighbourhood.

I would like to take this opportunity to thank the magazines, newspapers and anthologies in which the essays featured in this collection first found life: Irish Central (US); UCC German Department (German translation by 81 Sprüche – Schibri-Verlag Berlin; Chinese translation by the Shanghai Writers' Association); *The Elysian: Creative Responses* (New Binary Press, UCC); The Museum of Childhood Ireland – Músaem Óige na hÉireann; *Irish Examiner*; *Evening Echo*; *Sunday Independent*; *Irish Independent*; *Irish Times*; *Croí na Lee Úibh Laoghaire*, 2023; *Holly Bough*; *Shanghai Daily* (Chinese translation by the Shanghai Writers' Association).

Walk With Me Along Pine Street

On my dawn walk this morning and I heading up the Skeety Bars Steps. I paused awhile at the corner of Pine Street.

*

This is a city of steps and steeples, more steps and steep hills. And above the heads of the merchant paupers and princes, the golden fish on Shandon casts a sceptical eye over the fishbowl that I call home.

Two channels of the River Lee insulate the city centre from generations of Northside/Southside rivalry. Two factions holding up mirrors to each other, reflecting carbon-copy monasteries, breweries, cathedrals, towers and bridges.

We don't call it the inner city, it's just plain downtown, and home for me is a spaghetti bowl of streets centring on the one called Devonshire. My family has lived and traded here since the Vikings. A busy little shop more social than commercial. And bivouacked in various nooks and crannies throughout the house, my parents, twelve children, a clatter of pets and a string of guests who came to dinner and stayed.

Outside, the streets were bustling, too, with families talking and taking air. Shawl-wrapped Mamie Murphy selling apples on Pope's Quay, Connie the Donkey hawking sawdust for soakage to publicans or to those who butchered, cured or filleted – O'Connell's beef, O'Sullivan's bacon or Charlo Quain's fresh

Photo: Mirrorpix/Reach Licensing.

mackerel, and O'Brien's the Greyhound Stadium, home of the creamiest porter this side of the Lee.

And each morning a new day would be heralded by the dawn chorus, the sound of the men of Blackpool and the Red City of Gurranabraher walking and whistling their way along our street and all the way down the docks to the Motown of Fords and Dunlop. But that was a long time ago, a time when people were buttoned up in the days before Velcro.

Without a blade of grass downtown, street soccer evolved into a sport of its own. You'd find us there every day after school, droves of *Downtown Dirty Faces*, red-faced and roaring, funting a ball up and down Pine Street – every boy, girl, cat and dog chasing an inflated pigskin. Toddlers tackled teenagers, and the dogs of the street always waiting on the wing to score on the rebound.

My dog Tshirt will always be remembered for her sensational equaliser with a diving header. Her snout drove the ball home past the corner of the post, into the back of the goal, rattling the back of the onion sack to a clatter of steel-clad shuttering across McKenzie's, enough to put Pelé in the shade. And with no set time limit, a game once lasted the whole summer – from June right through to September. The final tally on the score sheet recording the decisive victory – 674 to 453.

But ashes to ashes, dust to dust. And flesh and bone gave way to rubber and steel. And all that remained was blood-drenched concrete and asphalt when a schoolboy's bones were crushed beneath the wheels of a truck.

With the death of a child, the people of downtown surrendered sovereignty of our streets. The families moved out soon after that, out to the reservations in the wastelands – and the heart of a city stopped beating.

And funny, that playground paradise that was Pine Street has long submitted to the developers' crushing ball. Where once the *Downtown Dirty Faces* played, now stands a multistorey car park, keeping the car safe from people. Yet on my dawn walk this morning and I heading up the Skeety Bars Steps, I paused awhile at the corner of Pine Street. In my mind's inner ear I swore I could still hear the shrieks of downtown dirty-faced delight. It's as if the ghosts of children past continue to play ball along the road. Still running wild, every boy, girl, cat and dog – quarter irons knocking sparks off the road, putting a pigskin squealing: rip, roaring, like a rocket rattling the back of the onion sack, sending shuddering waves along McKenzie's gate.

Beara

The self-obsession of childhood into late teens is probably the most highly tuned survival tool we humans have in our evolutionary armoury as we propel ourselves forward, fine-tuning our gene pool for future generations of the species. Human children tend to stay close to the nest for up to twenty years. Observers have recorded fascinating examples of some human offspring returning home up to thirty years after birth to be fed or have their laundry done. But the fact remains that most other animals must fend for themselves very soon after birth. In many cases, such as the wild Atlantic salmon and the sea turtle, the newborn come into this world alone, their parents having long since left the scene and skedaddled for the high seas.

This self-obsession of childhood probably explains why we are usually mature adults before we realise the extent of our parents' selflessness. And it's a hard fact of life that we are usually closer to old age before we acknowledge that, long before our parents met and came together as a unit to give birth and nurture us, they were individuals in their own right. It can be challenging to view our parents as individuals with dreams and ambitions who set aside their own personal aspirations to invest their hopes in a new generation. Alas, for many, by the time the truth dawns, it's too late to acknowledge their sacrifice.

And so I sometimes think of my mother. Born into a family of ten sisters on a hilltop farm in Adrigole, Beara. It was a time before electrification, indoor plumbing or running water. As a young woman she left the splendid isolation and financial restrictions of her family's smallholding and moved to Cork city. By the time I was born and became aware of her, she had married my father, they had twelve children, and were trading from our small shop here in the spaghetti bowl of downtown Cork city. And so my world revolved around my parents, my eleven siblings, our shop, our neighbourhood and an exponential number of relations who seemed to dip in and out of our domestic life – it was the only reality I knew.

Such is the self-obsession of childhood, I never took the time to consider my mother and father may have had their own independent realities before that time.

*

My mother never spoke about loneliness. But on summer evenings she would look westward, and her heart would sink as the setting sun faded behind this urban horizon of cracked chimney pots and slate-clad buckled beams. Her mind would carry her west, out of the city and all the way to a hillside farm on the Beara Peninsula, where she and her nine sisters were born and reared.

She sometimes spoke of crystal-clear mountain lakes, sparkling like sapphires along the craggy spine that runs the full length of the peninsula, all the way to the copper mines that sweep down to the white sands at Allihies. She said Beara had a coast of breathtaking beauty, a dramatic shoreline carved by the pounding of the wild Atlantic Ocean, and kissed by the warm stream from the Gulf of Mexico bringing with it a hint of subtropical paradise.

By contrast, downtown Cork city, where I grew up, might as well have been a thousand miles away from the crashing waves, the rolling hills and the intoxicating solitude of Beara. My home

All roads lead to Beara.

was an extremely busy household – twelve children, my mother and father, two aunts and a string of guests who came to dinner and stayed. And, as if that wasn't hectic enough, our front room had been converted into a corner shop some time back in the late 1800s, so the door was always open, making our home a very public house, with people coming and going, morning, noon and night.

– It's like Piccadilly Circus, my mother used to say.

As a child I assumed she was referring to a circus of the three-ringed variety, with clowns, juggling acts, trapeze and performing animals – and that somehow made total sense to me.

And sometimes my father would recognise that faraway look in her eyes, and though it would be late in the evening he would pile us all into the car. We'd strike the road west to Adrigole on the Beara Peninsula, a long road back then. Once there, we would visit my cousins and my mother's sisters Kit and Dinah, often swinging by Cappaleigh to visit her Aunty Mamie. And then the return journey, arriving back home to Cork in the early hours before a new day dawned, in time to open the shop the following morning.

We didn't do family holidays, but for me there is one holiday that stands head and shoulders above all the rest. Looking back on that time, I now assume my mother in her own way was attempting to indoctrinate this downtown city boy into the Beara way, and I am eternally grateful.

I was nine years of age going on ninety; past the age of reason and wise beyond my years. I remember it well: my Auntie Kit came east to visit my mother in Cork, and like an East/West prisoner exchange at Checkpoint Charlie, I travelled west to spend the week with my Uncle Jack.

I remember that first morning in Beara. Peering from my bedroom window, I was struck by the clarity of the light, the expanse of the landscape, and the silence. South of the house, a patchwork of sweeping fields crisscrossed by stone walls built by generations of bare Beara hands – walls that led all the way down to the Atlantic Ocean and Bantry Bay.

Me and Uncle Jack quickly established a comfortable rhythm around the house. My first task each morning was to release the hens and collect the eggs while Uncle Jack busied himself tacking the horse with bridle and harness. Then the unmistakable sound from out back of the house – steel-shod hooves and iron-clad wheels on stone as Uncle Jack prepared for the road east, and with a hop, skip and most almighty jump, I'd launch myself up onto the cart next to Uncle Jack and we'd trundle out of the yard.

Shep the dog, weary of keeping pace, would leap on board and snuggle in between us. And that's how our day began, the three amigos heading east towards Johnny the Cross with our cargo, a churn of freshly squeezed creamy milk.

The barn bulging with that season's hay, Uncle Jack turned his hand to draining the boggy field, north of the house. Channels were dug and backfilled with stone: large rocks first, followed in decreasing size down to gravel in a tradition that had been handed down from father to son since Neolithic times.

Each day with Uncle Jack was an adventure, like that time we were herding cattle along the road. I was Billy the Kid on point, with the sole task of guiding the herd of five cows left into the yard. But the wise old Kerry Cow realised that the Kid was but a boy and challenged my authority. In my moment of hesitation, the Kerry Cow took the initiative and turned right.

– Go north of her! shouted Uncle Jack. – Go north!

– Which is my north-hand side? I roared.

Uncle Jack just laughed, and the Kerry Cow, in her own confident and defiant way, broke ranks and walked past me in the direction of Castletownbere.

Later, in his own philosophical way, Uncle Jack analysed the day.

— The confusion with using left-hand side and right-hand side is that it changes depending on the direction you are facing, he explained. — But the points of the compass always remain constant. You see, the points of a compass radiate from a fixed centre. The trick to finding a true direction in this world is to remain centred, he said.

Me, my Uncle Jack and Shep sitting on the stone wall south of the house, that's where you'd find us, every evening when the day's work was done. Sometimes, Uncle Jack would talk. Sometimes, he would listen. Sometimes, the solitude remained intact until he sang a verse of a song, *Silver Threads Among the Gold.*

On one such evening, just as darkness was coming in, I pointed to the headland on the far side of Bantry Bay.

— What's that over there, Uncle Jack?

— That's Sheep's Head, he said.

— And is Sheep's Head a nice place, Uncle Jack?

— Sheep's Head is one of the nicest places on this earth, he said. — I hear it's almost as nice as Beara.

And that was the magic of Uncle Jack. Like the points of the compass, my Uncle Jack was centred. Beara was his universe, and he instilled in me the importance of sense of place and a love of parish.

Night after night I'd sit on that low stone wall, transported to a magical world by tales of the townland: piracy, the Spanish Armada and how Wolfe Tone guided the French fleet into these waters. He told of his namesake, Michael O'Shea, and the gallant rescue off Calf Rock, and the bizarre story of Mick Kelly, the only man with the distinction of smoking a pipe at his own funeral …

— This is Beara, he'd say.

He conjured up a mystical land where the Demon Hound of Lough Avoul warned of impending doom, and the lonesome cry of the *bean sí* swept along the crest of Crooha, from Leitrim Beg all the way down into Kilcatherine. This is Beara, where the last clan of the Ancient Gaelic Order made their stand against the English Crown at Dunboy. This is Beara, where the finest gentlemen of Queen Elizabeth's court, Captain John Bostock and Commander George Carew, crossed Dursey Sound and wilfully slaughtered three hundred women, children and elderly. This is Beara, where O'Sullivan Beare led the remnants of his people on an epic march to Leitrim, and only a handful survived to tell the tale. This is Beara, where the mountain ram is the king of all that he surveys, and the regal splendour of the ancient *Cailleach* is the queen of the Corca Dhuibhne and the Corca Laoigdhe. This is a land where history and story go hand in hand, fact and fiction dovetail seamlessly, and the spiritual and the natural complement each other without contradiction or contrivance. This is Beara, a land shaped by the people and a people shaped by the land.

And every evening drew to a close with Uncle Jack's immortal words,

— You go up and make sure the chickens are safe from Mr Fox. I'll go in and warm some milk and honey.

This is Beara, the land of milk and honey.

NOTE

This essay was first published by Irish Central (US) and *Irish Examiner* (Ireland). The poem *Come West With Me to Beara* by Cónal Creedon was subsequently written and first presented as spoken-word poetry, accompanied by Eva McMullan and Crosshaven Community Choir at Garnish Island and Bere Island during the summer of 2023.

Come West With Me to Beara

She seldom spoke of loneliness –
but sometimes dared to dream.
Up high. Up high. Where Golden Fish and Angels fly.
And the setting sun reached back to say:
Come west the road with me.

She dared to dream of crystal stream.
Thro' cracked chimney pots – slate-clad buckled beam.
From Barley Lake – along craggy spine,
past clear pools sparkling blue,
sweeping down to white sands at Puxley's mine.

She dared to dream of townland tales:
the gallant rescue off Calf Rock,
the Spanish Armada – when the Ranties had their day.
And Wolfe Tone led the French
in treacherous water – against the tide of Beara Bay.

This is Beara, she'd say – where the ancient Gaelic order
stood against the Crown at Dunboy Bay.
A shoreline of breathtaking beauty,
carved by the pounding of the wild Atlantic,
and kissed by the warm stream from Mexico way.

This is Beara – where the finest gentlemen of Queen Elizabeth's court:
Captain John Bostock under George Carew,
crossed Dursey Sound to the island sanctuary
and wilfully slaughtered the innocent,
thrown from the cliff face – two by two.

This is Beara – a marriage of fact and fiction.
Where the spiritual complements the natural
without contrivance or contradiction
And O'Sullivan Beare led the remnants of his clan
On the *trail of tears* to Leitrim – from this – his homeland.

This is Beara – a mystical land.
Where history and story go hand in hand.
Where the Demon Hound of Lough Avoul
warned of impending doom,
and the lonesome cry of the *bean sí* sweeps along the crest of Croo'.

This is Beara – a land shaped by the people,
A people shaped by the land.
where the mountain ram is king of all that he surveys,
and the regal splendour of the ancient *Cailleach*
is crowned queen of the Corca Dí and the Corca Laoigdhe.

So, no. She seldom spoke of loneliness,
but sometimes dared to dream.
Up high. Up high. Where Golden Fish and Angels fly.
When the setting sun reached back to say:
This is Beara – come home the road to me …

Rossmuc

We're On the One Road by the Wolfe Tones crackled from the car radio.

Funny how a song can dig deep into the crevasses of the cranium to unearth a long-forgotten past.

*

Like wildfire, the rumours had spread around the schoolyard, and that's what prompted Jojo Duggan to raise his hand and ask a simple and straightforward question.

— Are we going on a school tour, Brother?

Brother Hennessy hesitated and looked out across the sea of faces, from desk to desk, past row after row of expectant eyes twinkling beneath fringe-cut bowl-cuts.

— Let me think about it, he said.

Sometimes the answer to a simple and straightforward question is neither simple nor straightforward.

For this twelve-year-old schoolboy, Ireland was a sepia-toned, wax-cloth map hanging in the classroom. We'd gather around it and rattle off the Irish national industrial centres.

— Carpets in Navan.

Sugar in Mallow.

Electricity in Ardnacrusha.

Like some aberration of reality, this New Ireland as envisioned by Seán Lemass presented a semi-state hybrid of an industrial-ised future firmly rooted in our pastoral past. Of course, there was that day Brother Hennessy asked,

— Right, Creedon — name the minerals found in Ireland.

— Fanta, 7UP and Tanora, Brother.

Nineteen-seventies Ireland was a rising tide and Cork was on the crest of a wave. The Motown of Ford and Dunlop was the powerhouse of the city – pumping steam. It was the era of the *job for life*, where a workplace was handed down from generation to generation, and we would be next in line to take our place on the assembly line.

Brother Hennessey had heard the whispering around the staffroom. Two of the rugby-playing, fee-paying colleges in the city were planning school tours. One had their sights set on Switzerland, the other on Paris. Two schools whose primary focus was educating the next generation of captains of industry, merchant princes and sons of the professional classes. By comparison, my alma mater, the North Monastery, boasted alumni from the vast, blue-collared heartland on the Northside of the city.

Celebrated in song and in story, the North Monastery was a nursery for hurlers and heroes. Past pupils had made their mark as poets and politicians, with pride of place dedicated to the *Real Taoiseach* Jack Lynch and our two martyred republican lord mayors, McCurtain and MacSwiney.

Brother Hennessy instinctively understood that working-class values came hand in hand with working-class wage packets. Therein lay the kernel of the conundrum: the expense of a school tour to Europe would be far beyond the financial reach of his flock.

That weekend Brother Hennessey set to work calling in favours. He secured a bus from Cronin's Coaches, a batch of Dolly Mixtures from Linehan's sweet factory, and Punches pledged a box of Tayto and a crate of Tanora. By Monday morning a plan was in place.

North Monastery class photograph, 1970.

— Right, says he. — We are going on a school tour.

A tsunami of excitement swept the classroom.

    — Paris? Switzerland, Brother?

    — No! says he. — Not Paris or Switzerland. We are going to
    Rosmuc!

    — Rosmuc, Brother?

Brother Hennessey nipped any hint of dissent in the bud saying,

    — Rosmuc was good enough for Patrick Pearse — it's good
    enough for us.

He went on to say,

    — Life is a bus journey. So, let the journey be our reward!

And so, on the appointed day, fifty-two wild boys and a Christian Brother piled onto a bus and trundled out of Cork, on the rocky road to Patrick Pearse's cottage in Galway. And yes, motion sickness induced a few cases of projectile vomiting, but it's fair to say that by the time we reached Limerick, communal supping from bottles of Tanora with a froth of Tayto flakes floating on top had established a collective antimicrobial immunity against measles, chickenpox, smallpox, leprosy and every known schoolboy infection.

Brother Hennessy mapped out a circuitous route tracing the footsteps of O'Sullivan Beare. At every crossroads and village he identified holy wells, burial grounds and ancient battlefields strung out along the blood-drenched road of Irish history – from Cork to Rosmuc.

Pearse's cottage, set in splendid isolation on the shores of Loch Oiriúlach, framed by the towering Twelve Bens and the majestic Maamturk Mountains, is a place of breathtaking beauty. This landscape inspired the *Patriot*, who in turn inspired the birth of our nation. Brother Hennessy impressed on us the significance of this magical place, with extracts from *Eoghainín na nÉan* and

Íosagán, finishing in an impassioned flourish with the prophetic words from Pearse's oration at the grave of O'Donovan Rossa:

— The fools, the fools, they have left us our Fenian dead.

The cottage was small and spartan, and with access limited to five individuals, Brother Hennessy organised us in batches. We were led in hushed tones from the sparse kitchen to the austerity of the bedroom – the only apparent furniture a small, iron-framed bed. When our guide announced that the Fenian Joseph Mary Plunkett's brother had stayed here with Pearse, it prompted Jojo Duggan to ask,

— In the same bed, Brother?

— Ah! Christ no, man! They took it in shifts.

But stunning scenery and the serenity of solitude offer little by way of entertainment to a busload of schoolboys, so we entertained ourselves with a game of Brits & Patriots – a new take on the old standard Cowboys & Indians. And maybe Dagenham Dave, the leader of the Brits, ended up in the lake as a reprisal for the burning of Cork, but what happens on school tour stays on school tour.

Maybe it was the sheer enthusiasm of Brother Hennessy, but something about that day spent in the wilds of Connemara was profoundly inspirational. Every mountain, bog and outcrop seemed to present a narrative and a profound understanding of what it meant to be Irish. Ireland was no longer just a jaded abstract map hanging in the classroom. For the first time in this boy's life, Brother Hennessey had succeeded in imparting a deep and meaningful interpretation of Ireland as a constantly evolving work in progress – an ancient land shaped by the people and a people shaped by the land.

And so, with the darkness of evening setting in, it was time for us to strike the long road home again; one final stop at

Salthill for sausages and chips and an opportunity to empty our pocket money into the slot machines of the amusement arcades along the waterfront.

And so, with the final diversion completed and all the necessary concluded, including a reminder to visit the facilities, it was time to head for home. A quick headcount and we were back on the rocky road to Cork. Brother Hennessy shortened our journey with a sing-song – the full republican repertoire, from '*Boolavogue*' to '*Seán South of Garryowen*'. But something about the rousing culturally inclusive lyrics of '*We're on the One Road*' just seemed to capture the spirit of that day. We sang it over and over again – from Salthill, County Galway all the way to the Burren in County Clare.

Half a century has passed, and yet the names and faces of each and every one of those boys on the bus that day is indelibly etched in my memory. Red-faced and carefree, singing at the top of our lungs, living in the present, mindfully in the moment – blissfully unaware that, within a decade, Ireland would be battered by a gale-force recession and Cork would be in the eye of the storm.

By 1985 the Monahan Road Motown of Ford and Dunlop had padlocked their gates, never to open again. Verolme dockyard had slung its hook and abandoned ship. This port town offered no safe haven. Dockers clocked out. For the first time in living memory the quayside remained silent, and a string of early-morning houses, from the Marina Bar to The Donkey's Ears, stacked their kegs by the quay wall for the last time. The city was on its knees.

With half the town unemployed and the other half redundant, the only career opportunity open to me and my classmates was to take the next Slattery's bus heading for London – and onwards to Brixton, Brisbane, Berlin, Boston or the Bronx. The day of the job for life was over.

And if *life is a bus journey*, as Brother Hennessy said, I sometimes think it's odd that me and the class of 1972 got on the same bus but, by the twists and turns of life, we all ended up in totally different places.

But sometimes, when faced with the challenges of life, I like to think that maybe in some alternative reality, that old Cronin's coach is still trundling along some back road between Rosmuc and Cork. Brother Hennessey is still driving on the sing-song. And a busload of schoolboys, high on Tayto and Tanora, singing as one, over and over again.

We're on the one road.
Maybe the wrong road.
But we're together now who cares.

Ballybunion

What a beautiful noise – coming up from the street …

Something about Neil Diamond transports me to another time, another place.

*

I'm ten years of age and the word Ballybunion resounds around inside my head with a mythical lilt, like Timbuktu and Transylvania. It sounds exotic, full of mysterious promise, a land of make-believe, a veritable dreamland, a fairyland – like Disneyland.

And even now, decades later, my memory conjures up an enchanting potpourri of sight, sound and scent. The bone rattling and racket of bumper cars – iron wheels on steel sheeting, a shower of sparks overhead and the aromatic blending of cordite, candyfloss and fish 'n' chips. A summertime melange of seagulls squawking, hawkers hawking and children squealing with delight – wrapped up in the freshest salt sea air wafting in off the wild Atlantic Ocean. And it all comes together in my mind as one almighty sensory orchestration that can be triggered by the opening strains of Neil Diamond,

 – What a beautiful noise – coming up from the street.

The Jewel of the Kingdom, I call it. Fellow Corkonians have been known to cast a glance of suspicion and derision in equal measure whenever I mention my fascination with Ballybunion. My disloyalty perceived as a hair's breadth short of treachery.

— Like, what's wrong with Goleen, Mizen, Inchydoney, Owenahincha, Allihies, Youghal and the other hundreds of acres of white-sand beaches here in Cork?

Alas, as is often the way with irrational obsession. I have no adequate explanation as to why I have such a profound attachment to this seaside town in faraway north Kerry. After all, I had only ever been there on a handful of occasions. It was so long ago that the memory has become misty with time. And yet the connection is deep and goes right down to the marrow of my soul.

Well last week, there I was standing on my street and who came along, only Theo – a childhood friend and neighbour. With a lifetime of shared history to our credit we always have plenty to talk about. So we did what we always do. Theo is a gifted conversationalist – witty, lyrical, poetic and a master at delivering a curly tale.

The conversation turned to times past, and the past is a funny place. My relationship with my past is complicated and at times contradictory. Sometimes, I wonder if my past and my future are part of some conflicting time-equilibrium paradox. Two fictional worlds precariously balanced on either side of the scales of myth and lore. The *future* speculates on what might be, while the *past* wallows in what might have been. The truth only exists in that very narrow band in the *present* – where both realities intersect.

Anyway, Theo was talking about my dad and a day trip to the seaside. It was a long time ago, sometime back in the last century – nay, it was back in the last millennium. And as often happens when processing the past, disparate episodes come together like pieces of a jigsaw to create one massive memorable picture. And that's the beauty of viewing the world in the rear-view mirror

– it presents 20/20 vision to a seamless continuum of edited episodes.

— Remember Neil Diamond, he said.

And he mouthed the first few bars of *What a beautiful noise comin' up from the street.* And just like that, I found myself transported in time. I was ten years of age, running through city streets with the *Downtown Dirty Faces.* Theo remarked that our two families, the Creedons and the McAuliffes, contributed seventeen children into a neighbourhood that was already densely populated by large families. A neighbourhood without parks, green fields or open spaces. And so, without as much as a blade of grass, the downtown streets of asphalt and concrete were the playgrounds of our childhood.

> — No summer camps for kids back then, he said. — No such thing as a crèche, and the notion of a family holiday was unheard of. But your da – Connie Pa Creedon – was a legend.

And though my opinion is informed by my natural bias, I did agree with Theo's observation. Not only was my dad interesting and interested, but he was also philosophical and funny. And when he wasn't entertaining the neighbours with his ham acting at the meat slicer of our little shop on Devonshire Street, he kept himself busy as a CIÉ bus driver. Connie Pa's daily travail was to travel the road between Cork and Ballybunion during the summer months. Characteristically witty, he once summarised his day's work as,

— Two skids and a jam-on.

Theo proceeded to weave a colourful tapestry of long-for-gotten memories. And with each escapade explored, the secret of my lifelong infatuation with that seaside town became unlocked. He told of how, with a nod and a wink, the word would go out across our street that there would be an unofficial special dispensation the following morning. And at the appointed time, my dad would pull up the bus at the corner of Pine Street. The hiss of the air brakes was our cue. He would stall the fifty-two-seater for just enough time to allow a swarm of downtown dirty-faced kids to pile onboard. Sandwiches wrapped and togs and towel rolled tight in Roches Stores bags, and we were off for a day to the seaside – from downtown Cork city streets all the way to wide-open spaces of Ballybunion in north County Kerry. Such were the perks of a CIÉ driver.

It was an endless journey over bent and buckled roads, through a landscape that seemed like a most magnificent colourful patchwork quilt – dotted with exotic-sounding townlands, parishes and place names: Mallow, Buttevant, Newmarket, Kanturk, Freemount, Rockchapel, Abbeyfeale, Listowel. Hours of driving along the highways and byways of north Cork before crossing into the Kingdom of Kerry.

It was a long time ago, fifty years ago or so. It was a time before Amazon or DHL parcel delivery. So retailers relied on the CIÉ bus to deliver packages along with their ticket-bearing passengers.

A bit like Wells Fargo staging posts in the Wild West – every crossroads, town and village had a bus office identifiable by a red-and-cream circular enamel CIÉ sign. These ad hoc parcel offices invariably operated as a dual purpose. For the most part they served as the local pub, but once the CIÉ bus pulled up outside the door, they transformed into an extremely busy parcel office. A parcel office that reverted to its original purpose the very moment the bus belched out of town.

Without doubt, Ireland was far more Catholic than Zen back then, but bus travellers seemed to channel their inner Buddhist in their enthusiasm for embracing the journey rather than anticipating the destination. And so at each stop, there would be a stampede of passengers off the bus and into the pub. In the time it took to manhandle the goods and chattels on and off and exchange the relevant paperwork, the commuters would engage in the conflicting practices of using the facilities and topping up with another quick drink.

Publicans quick to notice a gap in the market had a counter-full of porter poured out in pints in anticipation of a busload of thirsty travellers. There are apocryphal tales of some travellers opting to stay behind supping pints as the bus upped stakes and moved on without them. The Cork-to-Ballybunion *Express* had a number of such interruptions strung out along the road like the beads on a rosary. There is the story of the young seminarian from Kanturk – he was travelling home to visit his mother before taking his final vows, by all accounts he never got beyond Mallow. They say he married the publican's daughter – but I digress.

It was a time before the invention of the iPhone, a time when singing was a national pastime, and people tended to entertain each other. And so by the time the wagon trundled into Rockchapel, a sing-song would be in full flight.

One after another, in a noble call, lead singers would make their way to the top of the bus. Their alcohol-induced stagger concealed as a swagger, and the odd crumple and collapse would be blamed on the state of the roads. And having found their balance, they'd belt out a popular ballad while a choir of soloists and shrinking violets would stir up the chorus with aplomb.

Somewhere in the creases of my brain I have a memory of one such journey. The bus hopping off the road. My dad flustered with a look of panic in his eyes. And as we came to stop in some town – maybe Abbeyfeale – he turned to make an announcement. In one fell swoop he called for order, decorum and moderation when he shouted the instruction down the bus:

– Order, lads! Order, lads! Order! I'm running mad late!

Ye only have time for a shot or a glass here.

The town of Listowel had its own attraction – each time he drove through the square and out the Ballybunion road, the word would ripple from seat to seat in a reverential whisper,

– That's John B's!

Some pointing to the window above the pub insisting,

– He's up there writing a play …

… causing the bus to sway on its axle as all those on the left-hand seats lurched and leaned across to look out the right-hand windows in the hope of catching a glimpse of the bard himself.

And so, inspired by my chat with Theo, I undertook a pilgrimage, a day trip to Ballybunion retracing my dad's bus route. Last Tuesday morning I set out from Cork, me and my little dog. We travelled deep into the beating heart of the Irish hinterland in search of the Hy-Brasil of my childhood.

Hand on heart, I was anxious – concerned that my childhood dream would be crushed beneath the stark honesty of reality. But I need not have worried, all my memories had stood the test of time and held true.

Ballybunion is a magical seaside town. It has it all: sand beaches, crashing waves, clifftops, sea arches and caves. And there, perched on a promontory at the end of the main street, the ancient Geraldine castle. It served as a stronghold of the Bonzons (Bunyan) family, who gave the town its name. A fortification standing sentinel on a precipice separating two distinct beaches – traditionally designated as the Men's Beach and the Ladies Beach, keeping the sexes apart in an echo of a long-gone binary world. And just around the headland there is a more secluded bathing area known as Nun's Beach.

The history of Ballybunion weaves an intricate latticework. Just north of the town where St Chonnla drew his sword and slew the mythical serpent, there stands the ruin of the twelfth-century Kilconly church. And south of the town Ballyeigh beach is remembered as the battlefield of one of the most vicious faction fights on record. By all accounts, on St John's Eve 1834 a fight broke out between local feuding families, most notably the Coolens, Lawlors, Blacks and Mulvihills. They went at it fists flying and shillelaghs swinging. Details vary but it's said that over three thousand combatants – men and women – joined in the fray, and when peace was finally restored over two hundred corpses lay strewn across the beach.

But the story of Ballybunion is not just a litany of fist and fury – when it comes to advances in modern technology, the town has guaranteed its place in the history books as the site of the first east–west, transatlantic, spoken-word radio transmission. The date was 30th March 1919. The simple message – *Hello Canada, Hello Canada* – beamed out from the Marconi Station in Ballybunion was picked up by a receiver two and a half thousand miles away in Louisburg, Cape Breton, Nova Scotia. And so international wireless communications history was made in those pioneering days, a far cry from the Zoom calls, Snapchats and voice mails of today.

And if it's old-time values and romance that capture your imagination? Well, there's something about the Lartigue monorail that epitomises that magical era of timelessness. Said to have been designed with the shifting sands of Sudan in mind, but for some reason a prototype was put into service in this area of north Kerry. As you'd expect, the story of the Lartigue has become a fundamental part of local lore. I was charmed by the story of the requirement to transport two calves when delivering a piano from Listowel to Ballybunion – the livestock carried as a counterbalance to the piano on the outward journey. Then redistributed, a calf on either side, to maintain equilibrium on the return trip. An inspired Ballybunion solution to a Ballybunion conundrum.

It was the writer Frank O'Connor who put forward the concept that every town in Ireland has an *age*. This *age* would reflect how old its inhabitants should be when they leave the town of their birth. Well, I'm inclined to think that every town in Ireland has an *age* that would reflect when one should visit a particular town. And if Ballybunion had such an *age*, Ballybunion is a children's paradise.

This is a comic-book seaside town of donkey rides, candy floss, spice and all things nice; shops and beach shacks well stocked with buckets and spades, beach balls and every floatation device known to children of all ages. And, of course, the sparkling jewel in the crown – a main street dotted with amusement arcades, chair-o-planes and bumpers.

Ballybunion is the perfect town for a bespoke family holiday – tailor-made to nip 'n' tuck and stretch to meet all budgets. Plenty of fresh-air activities to keep the young ones occupied, and with the seaweed baths, hilltop walks and the odd round of golf there's enough to keep the old folks off their devices – while the young kids play and frolic and do what young kids should be doing, inspired by a most amazing natural seascape.

And so me and my little dog went for a wander from beach to beach to beach, around by the seaweed baths, up over the headlands, past the castle and across the dunes. And maybe my memory of this town has always been enhanced by the fuchsia-tinted lenses of nostalgia. But, as I retraced the steps of my childhood, it occurred to me that the natural beauty of this place is undeniable.

And so I wandered along Main Street, each sight, sound and scent triggering vignettes of a long-forgotten past. In the middle of the town I paused awhile at the Coast Café. The traditional cottage exterior preserved and intact since my previous visit half a century ago – the interior updated with a sensitive makeover and in keeping with the times – a new menu for a new generation of visitors.

I seem to remember this place with an old flagstone floor, a house where dinner was served in the middle of the day. In my mind's eye I can see my dad with the men of the town gathered around an old black-and-white telly. They're shouting at us to,

– *Whisht!* and – *Shuuush!*

Call it extortion, call it a protection racket, but they seemed happy to dole out shillings and half-crowns as payola to us – and we were happy to clear off to the amusement arcade and give them a bit of peace to watch the All-Ireland final. And that seems like a fair deal to me. And as I struggled to put a date on that particular memory, I believe it was that fateful year that Tony McTague (born in Clonakilty, County Cork) captained Offaly against Kerry. It was an epic battle that ended in a 16-all draw – both sides lived to tell the tale and fight another day. And when the dust settled the following Sunday, Kerry brought the silverware home to the Kingdom.

The recollections of childhood were coming at me fast and furious – I seem to recollect that, later that afternoon, me and my dad and the *Downtown Dirty Faces* regrouped back on that old CIÉ bus. We were drinking flasks of tea and eating cheese sandwiches and generally having a laugh. But the sound of the music and the allure of flashing lights from the amusement arcade was proving difficult to resist. That's when one of the lads, maybe Theo himself, made the observation:

    — How come? he asked. — How come we call 'em *bumpers* and the English call 'em *dodgems*?

My dad paused for a second or two.

    — That's what's known as *National Identity*, he said. — We Irish are inclined to go for it and drive on regardless — while our nearest neighbours, the English, are inclined to step back and dodge it. *National Identity* is all about perspective. How we present ourselves and how others perceive us to be.

And so my day trip back to my childhood was nearly done, but before I struck the road back to Cork, I dropped into the Pavilion Arcade – one last go on the bumpers for old-time's sake. Funny, they were beaming out the sounds of Robbie Williams, yet in my mind all I could still hear was the opening bars of Neil Diamond,

    — *What a beautiful noise …*

Ballybunion revisited – I was right back there. Back to a time when summers were hot and endless, running wild with the *Downtown Dirty Faces* – like I was trapped in an endless loop of memories of a magical childhood excursion to Ballybunion. And there's something about the bone-rattling of the bumpers, the scent of cordite and the shower of sparks overhead. And I'm zipping around, squealing with delight, driving on, pedal to the metal, head on, full force, ploughing into any bumper car that came within an asses roar of me. That's when a nimble-footed attendant took his life in his hands, and with a hop, skip and almighty jump he perched himself onto the back surround of my car. He tapped me on the shoulder saying,

— Cop on will ya! Stop bumping into people! Act your age!

Well, that was me told, it was time for me to grow up and go home. The times they are a changin'.

And as I drove home that night, the warm glow of the setting sun in my rear-view mirror, it crossed my mind that maybe my past will always be a pure fabrication of what might have been. Like Timbuktu and Transylvania, maybe Ballybunion is but a figment of my childhood imagination. But my memories are mine – and, fact or fiction, no one can take them away from me.

And yet, to this day, I can still see my dad. He glances in the mirror, his fifty-two-seater almost airborne hopping off the road – trying to make up time. He turns with a panicked look in his eyes. He's calling out for,

— Order, lads! Order, lads! Order! I'm running mad late!

Ye only have time for a shot or a glass here.

Cónal and Dogeen. Photo: John Minihan.

My Dog Dogeen

My grand-uncle Jeremiah had a *charm on dogs*. He lived in what was known as the Butter House, a small *síbín* in the heart of Inchigeelagh village. His was a life of prayer and frugal humility, a life he shared with his sole companion, a blue-eyed collie named Princess.

The old people around here tell me that my father also had a *charm on dogs*. And sure enough, every now and then an old sepia-toned photograph of my father will surface – jet-black hair, youthful eyes twinkling and smiling, standing there, and more often than not with some dog held casually yet comfortably in his arms.

I'm reluctant to proclaim my own *charm on dogs* – it's an accolade that demands third-party confirmation and endorsement. But now, as I enter my final quadrant, it is true to say that ever since boyhood, throughout the long and winding road of life – just as Fionn mac Cumhaill had Bran and Sceólang, I have always had a dog by my side.

Maybe I'm guilty of finger-wagging whataboutery, but the new normal of Covid-tide has insidiously permeated every aspect of life, not least the natural order and organic nature of dog ownership.

Yet there was something primordially magical when social restrictions caused society to redefine itself. It seemed like the most natural thing in the world when social interaction was cancelled and we contracted into small, tribal family groups. *Bubble* was the word coined to express this new social reordering. And within our respective *bubbles* the nation went dog crazy. It was as if we channelled our ancient hunter-gatherer instincts, each New Age nuclear family confined by the 2km travel restriction stalking our territory in circles with a mandatory mutt on tow. Overnight we became textbook experts in every canine breed created by man. And so the search began for a bespoke, non-shedding, hypo-allergenic, low-maintenance perfect pedigree. I found it interesting that prior to the advent of Covid, the term *non-shedding* was usually reserved for Christmas trees.

Staycation became a buzzword, and with a dog in the back seat of every family car, *dog-friendly* became the hottest ticket on Airbnb. Now don't get me wrong – throughout my life I have nurtured close and special relationships with certain hotels, pubs and restaurants. From time to time they oblige and allow my dog to come in out of the elements – sometimes they even put out an ashtray of water. These non-contractual arrangements had been established over time through a mutual relationship formed on trust and respect – never assumed as a right and always accepted on the understanding that the privilege could be withdrawn at a moment's notice without prior justification, vindication or explanation.

But ever since *dog-friendly* became another box to tick on Tripadvisor, what once was a very special concession has overnight become an entitlement. So much so that, recently, me and my dogeen made a hasty retreat from one such establishment – when the most unmerciful dogfight erupted between a labradoodle and a cockapoodle – skin and hair of the non-shedding variety flying. Meanwhile, the newly converted dog owners were indulging in a high-stool day, supping cocktails, lamenting that Covid has curtailed their annual run to the sun, and insisting that if Ireland had weather they'd never go abroad. So, I whispered a silent prayer for more rain.

But maybe the big wheel of life is turning. Maybe now that Covid is on the wane, the need to accessorise with a puppy might abate. Anecdotally, my local vet recently mentioned his difficulty in finding homes for a litter of Jack Russells. He added that this time last year the same pups would fetch 500 euro a pop,

    – But now that the social isolation of Covid has been lifted, you can't give them away for love nor money.

Anyway …

My little dog died last Monday morning. Her name was Jude – but here in the spaghetti bowl she was known simply as Dogeen.

Of course, my heartfelt empathy will always be reserved for the pain of human suffering across the planet and, closer to home, the death of a child or those near and dear to us will plunge the heartache of grief to the darkest, unfathomable depths. So I am reluctant to humanise or eulogise the passing of a family pet. But the fact of the matter remains that when word of Dogeen's demise filtered out onto the streets of this town, it prompted a collective wave of heartfelt emotion.

Jude's health had visibly deteriorated in recent months, yet nothing could have prepared us for the profound sadness that consumed our home following the finality of her last breath. Anyone who has lost a family pet will know the score.

Jude has always had a very special bond with my partner in life, Fiona O'Toole, so there was a certain consolation knowing that our little dogeen surrendered to the inevitability of death in her happy place – snuggled up, wrapped in a blanket in Fiona's arms.

Her early life was shrouded in mystery – like Victor Laszlo in *Casablanca*, Jude arrived to us without papers. She presented herself as a chocolate-eyed, button-nosed, biscuit-brown Border Terrier lookalike. Bordering on aloof, she ploughed her own furrow and marched to the beat of her own drum. Strong-willed but blessed with the sweetest temperament, Jude was the neatest little dogeen: self-contained, daft as a platypus, cute as a daisy.

Deaf as a doornail and extremely short-sighted, yet with the confidence of a superhero, Jude tapped into her own secret strengths – philosophical and stoical. She took everything life threw at her in her stride and on her own terms – it was her way or no way at all, and within days she had us fully house-trained.

I've heard it said, – Why keep a dog if you must bark yourself? Well, Jude never barked. Some suggested she was mute; I like to think she lived her life in silent contemplation. Although, on occasion, she was known to make a *meow* sound, and it crossed my mind that maybe she identified as a cat – most comfortable channelling her inner feline.

Within a week of her arrival Jude had made the neighbourhood – this world of shopkeepers, hawkers, coffeeshops and traders – her home. In those halcyon pre-Covid days, Jude regularly wandered up the street to Sin É or The Corner House. That's where you'd find her perched on a high stool enjoying the company and teatime tunes. A glass-half-full sort of dog – always bright-eyed and bushy tailed. And at closing time she had a nose for sniffing out a lock-in. But most of all she was happiest just hanging out with me and Fiona. She bore witness to every aspect of our life, for better or worse, the happy and the sad, the rich and the poor, the good and the bad – but never judgemental. And maybe that is the true blessing of a family pet: their very presence offers a practical insight and perspective of *Rotha Mór an tSaoil* – that paves the way for an acceptance of our own mortality.

Hand on heart, I have never actively wanted a dog, and I certainly never paid for one – they just seem to find me. Before Jude there was Patsy, named after the Cork City FC player Patsy Freyne. She had the sweetest temperament; blind from birth, yet never expressed any awareness of her disability. A philosophical, stoical dog who just took life in her stride.

Then there was Finbarr. Her mother was a corgi and her father was from Rathpeacon, and I'll leave it at that. Finbarr was the happiest dog in the world: she literally smiled her way through life. Back in the 1990s she was a star of RTÉ's children's television programme *The Swamp* – with an ego to match. And yes, the shaggy dog story is true. There was an occasion when a taxi arrived at the door of my launderette, sent by RTÉ to collect Finbarr.

— Taxi for Finbarr Creedon, said the driver.

She hopped into the back seat, and off she went like the Queen Mother, chauffeur-driven across town to the studio. Very soon after that a note was posted in the RTÉ canteen which stated:

NO TAXIS FOR
Goldfish, parrots, budgies, cats, kittens or pigeons.
And categorically,
No taxis for Finbarr Creedon.
Signed: *Management.*

Dogs come and dogs go. But their passing is invariably marked by heartache and a solemn vow to never again invite into my life such an emotional attachment with the inevitable pain of loss. Yet, as if preordained by some greater power, no sooner has one dog's bedding been dumped in the landfill when a new bundle of furry joy somehow manages to inveigle her paws under my table and into my heart. And so I fall in love all over again. But the first cut is the deepest.

Let me tell you about Tshirt. She was a husky of undetermined parentage. I remember it like it was yesterday. It was my Confirmation and my sister Rosaleen arrived down from Dublin with the cutest little puppy dog. Tshirt was her name. From that very first moment, when she jumped up into my arms, I was smitten.

Me and Tshirt were inseparable. We rode with Jesse James across the western plains. We defended Cork from the Vikings. We drove the Black and Tans back across the Irish Sea, like St Patrick drove out the vermin. And will I ever forget that day on Pine Street when me and Tshirt scored the winning goal in the FA Cup final.

The score: 17–All. The Angelus bell was calling us in for our tea. I caught the ball on the volley, sending it in low and hard across the goalmouth. Tshirt darted in from the wing and drove the winning goal home with her snout, sending a rattling racket along the steel shuttering of McKenzie's gate.

Tshirt was one of the pack, and each day she'd be waiting for me at the school gate – happiest running through city streets with the *Downtown Dirty Faces*. Every day with Tshirt was an adventure.

Now, there was that time …

Twelve o'clock Mass, St Mary's was packed to the rafters. At the back of the church the usual throng of bare-headed men huddled in the vestibule. Up front, additional rows of seating placed inside the altar to accommodate the overflow. And that's where I was that particular Sunday: seated on the altar – nearer my God to thee. Fr Moynihan, a commanding orator, was in full flight. He was identifying the subtle difference between communism and Christianity: both life choices would lead to poverty, but one offered everlasting happiness, while the other guaranteed an eternity of hellfire and damnation – it was a no-brainer.

A minor kerfuffle emanating from down by the holy-water font went unnoticed. But that's when I saw it. Tshirt's bushy tail swaying in the air, like a swath of pampas grass, waving its way up and down the centre aisle. Her whining of anxiety rising in pitch and frequency caused an escalation of consternation among the congregation. Fr Moynihan drove on with his eulogy despite all adversity. Tshirt reached the altar and stood erect on her hind legs. When she saw me it was like the cry of the banshee. And with a hop, skip and most unmerciful jump she was inside altar rail, doing helicopter spins across the polished marble floor in front of the tabernacle. Then, howling and yelping, she cleared the front row of seats and leapt into my arms.

– Lord God Almighty! roared Fr Moynihan. – You!

His voice echoed from nave to sacristy. Then, pointing his knuckled finger in our direction,

– You! he said it again. – Take your beast and leave the house of God this instant!

Me and Tshirt walked the walk of shame down the centre aisle and out onto Pope's Quay. We headed home, our fate and our faith in the balance. But, even at that young age, I knew that life was long and eventually I would make my peace with God, and the fear of the burning fires of hell was too far off in the future to worry about. My greatest concern was how would I explain to my mother that me and Tshirt had been excommunicated.

Excommunication had been doing the rounds in our house ever since my father's cousin Red Mick Riordan the Communist had made his stand and parted ways with Rome. I worried how my mother would react to the news that me and Tshirt would be joining cousin Mick on a one-way ticket to eternal damnation.

For weeks we waited as the sharpened blade of the excommunicator's axe swung above our heads, but no disciplinary sanction came from Rome. It seems that Fr Moynihan made a unilateral decision to grant a reprieve. The whole episode was hushed up, swept under the carpet.

— What the Pope don't know won't bother him, my dad said.

It's a sad fact of life that we humans tend to outlive our canine soulmates.

And many years later, when T-Shirt died, I cried. I cried because I was saying goodbye to my friend, and I cried because I was saying goodbye to my childhood.

At sixteen years of age, a boy struggling with the demands of manhood, there I was sitting at the turn of the stairs sobbing uncontrollably. That's when I noticed my dad.

— Are you okay, Cónal-een? he whispered.

I struggled to stem the tears and attempted to answer. But every emotion that had been locked in my soul had become knotted in my chest, preventing me from uttering a word. That's when my dad told me about Uncle Jeremiah.

— Uncle Jeremiah was just like you, he had a *charm on dogs*, he said.

He said that the night Uncle Jeremiah died, his trusty companion Princess, the old blue-eyed collie, made her way into the middle of the village and, turning to the moon, she howled out a lonesome and solitary lament. Princess's plaintive cry was her way of saying goodbye to Jeremiah and, just like that, the word went out across the land that Uncle Jeremiah had died.

But then the strangest thing happened: one by one every dog in the village echoed her sadness. And, gradually, the sound of grieving dogs spread beyond the village, from farmyard to farmyard. East to Toons Bridge all the way to the Gearagh, from Kilmichael to Gougane, and west beyond Timmy Johnny's, past Ballingeary. From townland to townland and parish to parish, the mournful sound of grieving dogs, like an orchestration of sadness, echoed from the hills that surround Uíbh Laoghaire. They cried right throughout the night until the first shaft of dawn's light announced a new morn.

    – They were saying goodbye to Uncle Jeremiah, he explained.

    – Goodbye to one they loved. Goodbye to one of their own.

That's when I noticed the glint of a tear in my father's eye. And it crossed my mind how a single expression of grief could conceal so many aspects of pain. I'm not sure if my father realised it or not, but he himself was also saying goodbye. Goodbye to his son. Because, within a year, I'd be taking a Slattery's bus to London. Goodbye to his boy on the cusp of manhood.

    – So, don't dry your tears, Cónal-een, he whispered. – It's good to cry …

And so we cried some more …

Mother of Invention –
Mistress of Innovation

I'm sure there is a medical term for my condition – but I prefer to just say that I'm a *giver-away-er*. All my life I have had a tendency to give away that which I hold most dear. My behaviour could be rationalised as an attempt to reconcile some internal conflict between ownership, possession and attachment. But regardless of why, the fact remains that as I travel through life I leave a trail of prized possessions in my wake – a bit like Napoleon's retreat from Russia.

It has been a recurring theme since childhood; a favourite toy soldier, a picture-sleeve Sex Pistols single, a signed copy of *Animal Farm*, a poster, a piece of art, a leather jacket – I once even gave away my car.

What is most confounding about these transactions is that they are never part of a trade or barter deal – I don't expect anything in return. More often than not, the beneficiary is likely to be an individual relatively unknown to me and possibly one I will never meet again. Ironically, the recipient usually has no vested interest, attachment, need or desire for my treasured trinket – in many cases my gift is perceived as a discarded cast-off – so it's safe to assume that my prized possessions probably end up in a charity shop or landfill.

But life has a knack of presenting a balance between *one hand* and *the other*. And while, *on the one hand*, I'm a giver – ironically, *on the other*, I'm a receiver. And though both trans-actions are mutually exclusive, it is fair to say that I receive far more than I give. I am constantly surprised by the kindness of people. On a subliminal level I receive an inordinate amount of encouragement and well-wishes. Sometimes it's as simple as a thumbs up, or a *Dowcha Boy!* from a passing taxi driver. Other times the engagement is more discerning and focused.

Well, last week while on holiday in Portugal, there I was stretched out on the sun lounger with nothing to occupy my mind but sea, sand and the thought of sizzling sardines for supper. So I turned to pondering the imponderables of life.

I began by reassuring myself that I'm not a hoarder by nature, but I had to concede that I do have a tendency to gather possessions around me. And over the years I have accumulated a diverse collection of objects, for the most part given to me by former neighbours. Families who had traded here for generations, and when the time came for them to finally shut shop and move on, they decided to give me a personal keepsake as a memento of their time living downtown.

So there I was taking the sun, and decided to engage the brain by compiling an inventory. Well, to start with, there is that collection of stained-glass fanlights from a local school, and they complement the pair of decorative glass doors from the former *Irish Times* office. Then there's Neilus O'Sullivan's weighing scales, and the framed *Terms and Conditions* from Malachy Skelly's betting office. There's the mirror from the hairdresser, the *prison art* sign from An Stad Café, a set of barbershop chairs and the last handmade sliotar in Cork. Then there's a number of small personal items from local pubs, coffee shops and tea houses, a few bits and pieces from my own launderette, and a handful of items salvaged from our family shop next door where I grew up.

But as the list expanded exponentially, my brain struggled to keep track of the eclectic inventory which included the under-taker's office chair, the framed hand-written poems from my friends Paddy Galvin, Theo Dorgan and Doireann Ní Ghríofa. And somewhere at the back of the cupboard there is that serving dish from the old Munster Hotel across the street. That's when I remembered the amazing piece of ceramic art I received from Carol Buckley up the street, and that reminded me of pieces given to me by the prisoners of Spike Island and Cork Prison, and the old punch-card factory time clock, not to mention the one hundred bricks from Murphy's brewery chimney that had been stored in Ned Ring's old blacksmith yard on John Street.

My mind filed through an endless yet incomplete, non-curated catalogue of wonderful artefacts. Maybe it was the Algarvian sunshine, or maybe it was a surge of pride, but I did feel a warmth well up inside when I realised that so many families from my neighbourhood had independently appointed me the custodian of some artefact from their time trading on this street.

My thoughts were momentarily distracted by the sound of new arrivals. A family unit on their holidays, fresh off the plane from Faro airport: mammy, daddy, two children – a boy and a girl. Each with hand luggage on tow like a wagon train trundling past the pool making a beeline for reception. Ah yes, that distinctive clickety-clack and whirring sound of rolling hand luggage.

But it occurred to me that I remember a time before the invention of hand luggage with wheels attached. I guess I have lived through the age of analogue before the days of digital. It was a time when the old-fashioned suitcase was the only luggage option available to the traveller.

I can see them now, generation after generation of Irish

emigrants, they are clambering onboard the *Innisfallen* or a Slattery's bus. Shiny suits and pockets full of dreams, they are leaving home, scattering to the eight corners of the earth, each and every one of them with a bulging suitcase bursting at the seams, held together by a trousers belt or a piece of old rope – it's an image indelibly etched into my brain.

But somewhere along the line the suitcase became extinct. And just like that, over night it was replaced by a hybrid combination of trolley and trunk, built to the precise specification of budget airlines' overhead cabin storage. This new form of *pull-along suitcase* is now known simply as hand luggage. And so, in every airport, bus terminal, train station and ferry port across the planet you'll see Tom, Dick and Harietta clipping along with one of those newfangled hybrid wheelie hand-luggage things on tow.

The more modern designs have four wheels, and last week in Faro airport I caught a glimpse of the future – an eight-wheeler stand-alone model. It occurred to me that, with the proliferation of e-scooters and Segways, it's only a matter of time before some bright spark comes up with a deluxe version of sit-on/ride-on hand luggage.

But here's the thing – for millennia we humans have been carrying bags and boxes on our backs – some cultures carry them on their heads. And though the wheel was invented 3,500 years ago, it took until 17th June 1973 before an enlightened individual came up with the idea of attaching a set of wheels to a suitcase.

And as I slapped on the factor-50, serenaded by the squawking of seagulls, I remembered a story my father told me about the invention of the *Pull-along Suitcase*, as it was known back then.

But first let me set the scene of what travel was like back in the golden age of air travel. A time when airports were glamorous and luxurious places. Travelling by aeroplane was a privilege enjoyed by the upper echelons of society: the wealthy elite, the stars of the silver screen and royalty. Airports were places to be seen in – even our own Cork airport was one of the hottest spots for the cool set. Thick-pile shag carpet. Bar staff: all brass buttons and dickie bows. Jazz at the Skyline Bar was the height of socialising sophistication, serving alcohol the full three-hundred-and-sixty-five days of the year including Christmas Day and Good Friday – it somehow seemed to put this place, not so much beyond the law but above the law. And the 747 Restaurant with a full wine licence and haute cuisine featuring smoked salmon and melon boats – the airport offered a taste of the 007 lifestyle.

For the price of a Babycham or Bacardi and Coke you could live the dream, rub shoulders with the jet set, and for a few hours on a Friday night pose at the bar and be that international man of mystery.

French doors led the way to the viewing platform, where the in-crowd could step out, Martini in hand, wave to their loved ones departing or coming in to land. But above all, the airport offered an escape for those of us who couldn't afford to leave an opportunity to bask in the reflected glamour of bone fide travellers. And as I lie here basking in the Portuguese sun, my mind conjuring up those days, it's difficult to imagine the extent of luxury and comfort offered by airports before the advent of mass tourism and the introduction of paper cups and plastic spoons.

But 9/11 was a game changer – intensified security meant endless queues, aggressive policing, body searches, removing shoes, fingerprints and eye scans, armed guards and sniffer dogs. Where once was a haven of hospitality has now been downgraded to outright hostility.

But *fadó, fadó* – way back in the good old days, there was no requirement for something as naff as wheels on a suitcase. Because there was always an ample supply of youthful muscle to fetch and carry the bags of the well-heeled. *Manhandle* was the term used to describe the work of *porters*. It seems the demise of the old-fashioned suitcase came hand in hand with the rise in popularity of budget airlines and the associated mass travel of the not-so-elite hoi polloi. The democratic reality of this broadening of the socio-economic band required that the great unwashed would carry their own bags.

And as my dad told it, a neighbour of ours was instrumental in developing the *Pull-along Suitcase*. Ned Ring, our local blacksmith, spent his days servicing the hoofs and shoeing the last of the Murphy's brewery dray horses. Without doubt the days of horse handlers of the nineteenth century were numbered. They struggled to remain valid in the twentieth century as they hurtled towards the new millennium and the dawn of the twenty-first century.

I remember Ned Ring. His son John, who played clarinet with the Butter Exchange Brass and Reed Band, was a boyhood friend of mine – we were in the same class in the North Mon. I enjoyed much of my well-spent youth in and around Dominic Street, John Redmond Street, Eason's Hill and the warren of lanes around Shandon under the watchful eye of the golden-fish weather vane that turned with every call of the wind. Maybe I'm mistaken, but I seem to remember that Ned Ring was a granduncle of the film actor Jonathan Rhys Meyers who grew up just around the corner on Dominic Street, but once again I digress ...

Back in the day, that stretch of city – John Street, Knapp's Square, Pine Street and Carroll's Quay, out along the Kiln River to Poulraddy and all the way to Blackpool – was a hive of light industry: coopers, brewers, carriage builders, sweet makers, distillers, dab and dowel merchants, panel beaters, coffin makers, and of course Paddy Daly's furniture yard a wonderland playground for generations of downtown dirty-faced kids – and there at the end of Lower John Street, Ned Ring's bellows-and-anvil blacksmith's forge – all fire and brimstone like Hades itself.

And there's something visceral about the hammering of steel on red-hot iron sending a shower of sparks flying, the hiss of steam as white-hot metal is plunged into the cooling barrel. Conjuring up the most brilliant conglomeration of sights and scents: steam rising from rain-soaked horses, iron-shod hooves – fire, black smoke and iron. It was like the alchemist's laboratory, a magical place, and that's where you'd find us after school.

Anyways – this is the story as my father told it. Seemingly, our elderly neighbour, Dolly McKay, originally from St John's Villas, was returning home to Cork having spent a lifetime living and working in London. Dolly's older brother Alec had planned to travel to the UK to assist his sister with the move. But as the day drew near, he realised that the massive suitcase required to carry all of Dolly's belongings, although manageable on the outward journey when empty, would be far too heavy to carry on the return journey when packed with all of Dolly's possessions.

Well, one morning Alec was explaining the conundrum to my dad at our shop counter when Ned Ring arrived in for a newspaper and a bottle of milk. Ned, who was a contemplative man, didn't say anything – he just listened. But when Alec finished saying what he had to say, that's when Ned spoke up. He had an idea that if they could attach a child's roller skate to the base of Alex's suitcase, it might solve the problem.

Later that night the men of our street gathered at Ned Ring's forge, and there, with only the glow from the blast furnace and a spray of sparks to light up the night, Ned set about designing a prototype. With a stick of chalk in hand he drew in precise detail the world's first *Pull-along Suitcase.* And after much cutting, grinding and sparks flying, Alma Dowling's roller skate was mounted onto a bracket and fixed to Alec's suitcase. Ned decided to attach an extended *collapsible* handle to the side –

    – Easier to pull, he said. – And it will add structural support where needed.

For the record, the date was 17th June 1973.

When the *Pull-along Suitcase* was eventually revealed to the neighbours, there was a collective sense of shock and awe. Some even giggled. Although all agreed that the collapsible handle was ingenious.

Alec was not convinced, saying that the English would only be laughing at him if he was seen pulling a suitcase with wheels through the streets of London.

    – Let 'em laugh! said my dad, – You'll have the last laugh, Alec boy!

And the rest as they say is history …

The old people on these streets say that Ned Ring could have made an absolute fortune if he had patented his design – but Ned insisted that the *Pull-along Suitcase* should be made available to the world free gratis without patent because it would further the cause of equality and help elevate the status of the working class.

    – That's the kind of man Ned Ring was, my dad said.

So there you have it, from the horse's mouth …

On this day back in 1973, the world's first *Pull-along Suitcase* was invented by Ned Ring on Lower John Street, here in Cork city, Ireland.

And there's a curly twist to this tale. Well sadly, sometime after that, Alec McKay died. His sister Dolly – who by that stage was heading into her nineties – decided her travelling days were well and truly over. And so, in 1979, when it was time for me to take the Slattery's bus to London and on to Canada, Dolly gave me Alec's *Pull-along Suitcase.* It's been one of my prized possessions ever since.

Ned Ring's invention changed the world, and for that we should all be grateful.

The prototype *Pull-along Suitcase* takes pride of place in my collection of neighbourhood artifacts – and who knows, maybe one day the Smithsonian might come calling …

But in the meantime – as my dad used to say,

– If necessity is the mother of invention,
laziness is the mistress of innovation.

Cornerboys

Since the invention of the teenager back in the 1950s, each successive generation has given rise to its own brand of youth culture: Teddy Boys, Rockers, Mods, Hippies, Skinheads, Bootboys, Punks, Rastas, Goths, Ravers and on and on, right up to Gen X, Y, Z.

As if fuelled by the rising sap of puberty, each new generation reinvents its predecessor. And although Ireland would never be considered a global trend-setter in the phenomenon of youth culture, from the late 1950s through to the early 1970s a unique indigenous group did emerge here – The Cornerboys.

Consider a time without televisions, a time when those lucky enough to have a TV set were limited to one black-and-white channel broadcasting for a few short hours each day and interrupted regularly by the official screencard stating: – *Is donagh linn an briseadh seo* (We apologise for the loss of transmission). Consider a time when families were large and accommodation was cramped. Consider a time before double glazing and central heating, when houses were cold, damp and draughty places. Well, back then, every crossroads, village, town and urban neighbourhood had a band of local Cornerboys. A gathering of brain and brawn, wit and halfwit. Each evening you'd find them gathered beneath the street lamp at the corner. Exposed to the elements in all seasons. Collars to the cold, Cornerboys huddled around the glow of a shared cigarette butt – holding court on their bleak corner that somehow offered an attractive alternative to a crowded house.

Outside Backwater Art Studio, Pine Street. ART TRAIL 1997.
Back: Julie Forrester, Catherine Hehir, Irene Murphy, Cónal Creedon.
Front: John Adams, Finbarr the Dog, Suzy O'Mullane, Maurice Desmond, Nickie Dowd.
Photo: Fiona O'Toole.

Down our street, the local Cornerboys stood out from all the rest, in that they did not, as the name suggests, congregate at a corner. You see, I was raised in a corner shop that had the geographical anomaly of being situated slap bang in the middle of the street, and that's where our Cornerboys would meet.

It is said that there is no life without light. Well, in my part of town there was hardly a light without life. Night after night, the yellow-cream glow from our shop window drew them like moths to a candle. Hanging out, sharing stories and cigarettes, and locking antlers as young bucks do.

I can see it now: the *Downtown Dirty Faces*, we're dancing on the street, celebrating Miah Dennehy's hat trick for Cork Hibs. Jojo Ryan's dad, heading home from his shift in Dunlop's, joins in the tarantella. He is lamenting an earlier generation of Cork soccer, saying,

— Rage Carter would have run rings around the lot of 'em.

— Not at all, Miah is the king!

— If Miah is the king, says Mr Ryan. — Long live the Republic!

Mr Ryan vanishes off into the misty coal smoke that always hung on Devonshire Street to a chorus of Cornerboys singing,

— Miah is the king! Miah is the king! Ee-i-adio, Miah is the king!

Backs to the wind, Cornerboys laugh, rub shoulders – hanging out, shooting the breeze was their thing. And with a whistle from some window or door, they'd peel off home for tea, only to return later and continue exactly where they left off, comfortable among their own until dusk became dark.

And, year after year, a new oral mythology would be created as the boys from Devonshire Street would head off on some campaign to see Manchester United or Glasgow Celtic, Cork in Croke Park, or following Cork Hibs to faraway Ballybofey. Sometimes forming brief alliances with lads from other corners across the Northside. I can hear it now,

— … if the Dominic Street boys are going, the boys from Devonshire Street will be there, too.

And on their return, the next year's history would be recorded with blow-by-blow accounts from the newly broken voices of the novices. Exotic tales of adventures in some distant land; epic stories of the wondrous things that they saw – black men, yellow men and men with towels on their heads, helmeted bobbies, red buses, underground trains, and how young Jimmy

Mullins would have been killed stone dead, only for big Georgie Buckley wading in –

– … took on fifteen of them all on his own, so he did!

As always the myth was larger than the man, and the man was but a boy.

It is said that there was no sex in Ireland before Gay Byrne. Of course, that doesn't explain families with exponential numbers of children. It doesn't explain the tragedy of Mother and Baby Homes. It doesn't explain the culture of domestic violence. It doesn't explain the horrific accounts of clerical abuse – but some would say that Gay Byrne, in his sometimes awkward way, tackled the thorny issues. Prior to Gay Byrne, all public debate and education of the masses was curated by the conservative controlling hand of the Catholic Church.

Sex education was limited to vague and confused references about birds and bees. For the most part, word of all things procreational was disseminated from street corners. The whisper of a dirty joke communicated a collective knowledge from the inner circle hardshaws to the younger lads on the periphery. A misinformed knowledge that they, in turn, were obliged to impart when promoted to that pride of place, with their backs to the wall. It was a regulated and filtered education where those too young to know were ordered out of earshot before the more in-depth analysis of the low-down nitty-gritty.

And, come nightfall, down our street the elderly and young slept peacefully in their beds, serenaded by the guffaws, laughter and caterwauling from the street below. They slept soundly, safe in the knowledge that the Cornerboys – our Cornerboys – were self-appointed sentinels, ever vigilant.

The Wanderers (1979), a film based on the novel by Richard Price though set in the Bronx of the early 1960s – captures a universal moment of youth culture – that watershed moment of a world teetering on the cusp of the television age. The story follows the exploits of a bunch of neighbourhood lads. Their universe centres on a corner and stretches to no more than a couple of streets away. They live a full life within tight, claustrophobic parameters: falling in love, forming friendships and defending their patch – totally oblivious to the greater outside world and the storm clouds brewing on the far-off horizon of Southeast Asia.

This Philip Kaufman film marks a time when grown boys are trapped in men's bodies, and no doubt it presents a romanticised version of reality. Then again, stereotypes and clichés exist because they reflect a truth.

I'm sure many would write off *The Wanderers* as lemon popsicle dipped in kitsch Americana, but there are redeemable aspects to this tale. Not least, its multi-stranded, character-driven narrative strung together with a powerfully evocative soundtrack.

What I find most intriguing is that juxtaposition between teenage nostalgia and brutal realism. Watch out for the sudden gear shift of two magical turning points towards the end of the film, when we are offered a window to a greater world – initially through a TV shop window as the news of an assassination in Dallas filters onto the street, and subsequently through the window of Radio City Music Hall in midtown Manhattan, where we see a young Bob Dylan singing *The Times They Are A-Changin'*. This is not the day the music died, but rather the day the tempo changed.

Getting back to the corner in the middle of Devonshire Street, it is not so easy to identify the day the tempo changed. Many factors contrived to draw the era to a close – the arrival of television obviously was a consideration, and maybe smaller families meant homes were not as overcrowded and were more comfortable, making it more conducive to stay in. But above all, the demise of the Cornerboys on our street coincided with the mass exodus of families from downtown Cork city to the outlying areas.

These days, from time to time, maybe at a bus stop, supermarket or football match, old Cornerboys' eyes meet and we nod in recognition at all that has passed. Sometimes we stop and chat, old myths are relived, and new myths are created.

And maybe there were some rough diamonds in our ranks, but they were our Cornerboys. And where I come from, a rough diamond will always be more precious than polished coal.

Changing Our God

Historians will swear blind that, back around the sixth century, St Finbarr founded Cork, and maybe he did. But the old people on our street tell it differently.

Seemingly, Finbarr set out from Dublin in the footsteps of St Patrick. He was heading south to Cork, but along the way, or so they say, he lost his way. He spent six months wandering around the Bog of Allen, living off wild mushrooms and berries. He fought off feral hedgehogs, rabbits and hares. As my dad put it,

— Aten' alive he was, by wazzies and midgies. Scarred and blistered from head to toe by gorse, nettle and blackthorn. What that man went through made an eternity in St Patrick's Purgatory seem like a week in Butlin's.

Starving, delirious, and just at that point when Finbarr thought God had forsaken him, didn't he poke his head through a gap in a bush at a place known locally as Finbarr's View. There laid out before him was the majestic, beautiful Lee Valley. His fading eyes focused on a bustling little market town on an island centred in a crystal-clear stream. Finbarr had found Cork. Or, as my dad put it,

— 'Twas a few lads from our street found Finbarr, and he was a lucky man that they did …

Legend has it that the saint spent his first night across the street where now stands the Ashley Hotel. Next morning, after a good night's sleep in a feather bed and a fine feed of pig's head, they brought the saint up our street, where my friend Jimmy Sullivan's great, great, great, great-grandfather – give or take a few greats – gave his holy head a cut and a shave. Because as my dad put it,

— When you're tryin' to persuade people to change something as fundamental as their gods, presentation is half the battle.

Anyway, what I'm getting to is – generations of us Creedons have been getting their hair cut by generations of O'Sullivans. As a young boy in short pants I'd arrive into Tommy with a note from my mother with the strict instruction,

— Let the bone be your guide.

Tommy would bridge the armrests with a plank and invite me to sit up. And there is something comforting knowing that long before I was born many of those dead and gone, including my grandfather, had sat on the very same board.

An intimacy develops between men in a barber shop. It's a place where we congregate without a smoke screen or a glass to hide behind, a place where heads meet, a place where great sporting moments become greater with every retelling and also-rans are still running. It's a place where boys become old men and old men become boys again.

But above all it's a place where men talk, and talk is free when treated with the confidentiality of a confessional. And every milestone of my life – be it my first day at school, my First Communion, my first dance, my first date, my first job – has always been marked by a visit to O'Sullivan's. It's a bit like a recurring rite of passage. There is a certain magic to a relationship that develops over generations, yet ours is a relationship that is seldom explored beyond the confines of the barber's chair. For the most part, Creedons and O'Sullivans only ever see eye to eye in a mirror.

Although there was that time, ten, fifteen years ago or so, when totally out of the blue, me and my dad went for a day's fishing with the O'Sullivans. I could ramble on about fishy tales and the ones that got away, but suffice to say it was a magical day – one of those you just file away.

And when all was said and done, it was just me and my dad driving home into the setting sun. He was glowing, in full flight, telling me all about the day St Finbarr was found in Cork. He said that Finbarr came with a mission: One Nation. One People. One God. But back then, we Corkonians had a god for every change in the weather, so Finbarr compromised and offered the Trinity package: Father, Son and Holy Ghost.

In a lull in the conversation, I asked my dad if he thought it was difficult for St Finbarr to convince the people of Cork to change their gods.

   – God's-sake, he said. Not-at-all!

   We Corkonians did not change our gods.

   We only changed their names.

Cónal Creedon with his niece Asha in Mrs O'Driscoll's toyshop, Shandon Street.

The Scenic Route Home

Downtown Cork city is like being centre stage in a West End musical. It's an animated warren of shops and arcades, inhabited by every class of shopkeeper, hawker and market trader you could imagine. It's a city of characters and chancers, performers and poseurs – and a wander through the streets is an education in itself.

It's true to say that I learned more about life and human nature on my walks home from school than I ever did in a classroom. Each journey an adventure, a voyage of discovery, an exploration that offered an opportunity to engage with the city and its people.

Many decades have passed since my school days, and yet that sense of wonderment is still indelibly etched deep into my very being. And so, after many decades, I found myself back at the school gate once again, waiting to collect my niece Asha – what a wonderful opportunity to re-engage with the city and reflect on a refresher course of life and human nature through a new set of eyes.

On the warm spring afternoons we usually head for Fitzgerald's Park – on occasion we've taken the open-top city bus tour with a view to imprinting the topography of the town, stopping off at Blackrock village for a wander around the castle and a picnic before hopping on the next scheduled bus. But warm spring afternoons are far and few between, so, on a typical damp Wednesday afternoon, our first port of call is Mary Rose in Cork's English Market for a hot chocolate. Then onward to the Kino Cinema for a game of ludo. Asha has been known to rearrange her dice to more favourable numbers while I'm momentarily distracted by some old black-and-white Japanese film flickering in the background – she has learned from the best.

> — You can't teach an old dog new tricks, says I. – But ten out of ten for trying!

With the darkness of evening coming in, we leave the Kino and make our way back across the flat of the city and swing by the Crawford Gallery to chat with friends and check out what's hanging on the walls. We usually pop in to say *Hello* to our favourite shopkeepers: John Breen in Waterstone's, Catriona in Oasis, Noelle in Peacock and Ruby, or Breda in Miss Daisy Blue, Paul in the Rave Cave, James in the Coal Quay. They all know Asha now, and she's very comfortable in and around the shops. I suppose, because I come from a family of shopkeepers, I value the connections with the downtown traders – and if for no other reason, it'll be handy for Asha in her teenage years to have a few ports of call around the town if she ever finds herself stuck for a bus fare home.

Cork is a city of steps and steeples, more steps and steep hills that stretch endlessly upwards in every direction from the deep bowl of downtown. If time is on our side I will offer the option of the scenic route.

We make our way up along Shandon Street, lamppost by lamppost until we reach Mrs O'Driscoll's magical toy shop. She is the Queen of Shandon Street and her shop a veritable Aladdin's Cave of flashing fairy lights where all that glitters is gold. Ever since I was in short pants, with my nose pressed against that toyshop window, it has been a landmark in this boy's imagination. And though our scenic route is a detour that brings us north rather than south – visiting Mrs O'Driscoll's toyshop is a highlight and has become a tradition. A tradition I began many years ago with Asha's older sister Ruby. Mrs O'Driscoll is such a sweet and special woman, she greets us with a lovely *one of our own* welcome, and before we leave she always has a little gift under the counter for the girls.

Mrs O'Driscoll died a few years ago. And both Asha and Ruby expressed genuine heartfelt sorrow when they heard the sad news. I remember how the word wound its way around the warren of lanes of Shandon and spread right across the hills of the Northside. Then seeping down along to the North Gate Bridge, the sad news of Mrs O'Driscoll's demise crossed onto the island of downtown Cork city, making its way shop counter by shop counter along the spine of the old town. From the North Gate Bridge to the South Gate Bridge, then up the steep climb of Barrack Street and into the Southside. And I, like everyone who heard the word of her passing, realised it was the end of an era. Mrs O'Driscoll will be so sadly missed by generations of this town. It's only now in retrospect I realise how privileged we were to be included and welcomed into her world.

Me and Asha leave Mrs O'Driscoll's with a bag of goodies and, passing under the steeplc of Shandon, we make one final stop in to Linehan's sweet factory. She raises an eyebrow of doubt when I tell her that Tony makes every clove rock in the whole wide world, a bit like the Santy Claus of the sweet world. Tony lets her into some of the closely guarded secrets of sweet-making – such as how they get the clove inside the cut cloves or how they print a name running the full length of a stick of rock. But most of all, Asha is impressed by the old-style mechanical machinery, the blast of the furnace, the bubbling sugar and the tradition of using a hurley to make the mix. She looks on in wonderment as Tony and Danny shape and mould the molten sugar by hand.

And while the batch is cooling, we stand around and natter, and before we leave, Tony always gives her a bag of Dolly Mixtures for the long walk home …

And as we amble from post to pillar, it's non-stop chatter about this and that and nothing at all. She might mention something about homework, to which I give a stock reply:

— Ah sur', missing the homework one night wouldn't be the end of the world, would it? It never did me no har-um …

And she'd laugh.

I sometimes fill the gaps in the gobbledegook with fanciful tales of my own school days, detailing a litany of escapades and how we tormented the teachers – with the old switching the desk routine, or the hiding in the wardrobe lark, or the shoes out the window caper and of course the most bold-faced and brazen of all, I recount that tale when we re-enacted Kilmichael and ambushed three Christian Brothers as they made their way along The Lodge to the monastery.

And that's the way we go, doing the Pana Shuffle, weaving in and out of winding streets and market stalls, crossing bridges and stopping to chunter with whoever, whenever we take the notion.

As I always say – our meander through the streets of downtown Cork is a bit like being in a musical. Maybe it's the sing-song sound of people talking, or the way Corkonians engage in a deep and meaningful way about nothing at all – but there is always a sense that at any moment the whole street could burst out into song …

Yep, the walk home from school is an education in itself – and me and my niece Asha are PhD students – figuring it out as we go along.

What's the News?

In this era of twenty-four-hour rolling news beamed in from the eight corners of the globe and hashtagged directly by a personalised algorithm to a smart device in your pocket, it's difficult to imagine a world without news.

But consider a world without internet; without social media, YouTube, Tiktok or Instagram. Imagine a time before the smartphone, when the smartest device available was the electric toaster. Well, that's the world into which I was born.

I came of age at a time when news was a scarce commodity. Back in the day, news was suspect and seditious, and so government information agencies curated and conveyed a suitable version to a news-hungry public. This singular source of broadcast media circumvented all voices of dissent and contradiction. The island of Ireland of my youth was insular and monocultural. We were – *One Country. One People. One News.* And, far from being ahead of our time, 1974 Ireland was all that Orwell's *1984* had predicted.

For the most part, news was drip-fed to the provinces from Dublin by the state broadcaster Radio Éireann. And each day, following a whispered recitation of the Angelus, the nation would stop whatever it was doing and cock an ear for the twelve o'clock, six o'clock and nine o'clock news. It was a time when *catching the news* was a national pastime.

I was very fortunate, I grew up behind the counter of a newsagent's shop. In our house newspapers and print media reigned supreme. And while broadcast news was presented by newsreaders, print media was fuelled by news journalists, and there is a difference. Because rather than a scripted government memo announced in plummy Montrose vowels, journalists offered debate and opinion that challenged and gradually chipped away at the cosy cartel of the Church and state monopoly of the airwaves.

And though the national broadsheets held mighty sway along our shop counter, nothing compared to the power of local evening news. There is something about the undiluted Cork-centric perspective of the *Evening Echo* that cut through the rhetoric and elevated the local voice of politics, sport and culture to the heart of the national debate.

For me, the golden age of print media will always be when the *Evening Echo* was compiled, printed and distributed from Patrick's Street. A news machine with its finger on the pulse of the downtown beating heart. It generated the palpable presence of larger-than-life, sometimes idiosyncratic journalists who frequented an array of eccentric public houses, creating a forum of engagement for the great unwashed and the fourth estate. This collision of wits and halfwits created yet another vibrant strand to the colourful tapestry of the city. It was a time of epic newspaper lore and mythical anecdotes – such as the apocryphal tale of a secret drink hatch that linked Le Chateau bar to the *Echo* print room on Faulkner's Lane.

Integral to the life cycle of the city, you could set your watch by the early afternoon surge of news literally exploding onto the streets as squadrons of Echo Boys raced from Bowling Green Street, heralded by the evocative sound of,

– E-eecho! Eve-a-ning E-eecho!

… bouncing off every bus stop, bridge and bank corner.

More than just a disseminator of news, the *Echo* has always contributed to the cultural uniqueness that is Cork.

In my mind's eye I can still see four generations of the Kelleher family selling papers at Falvey's Corner, small change stacked in columns along the chemist's windowsill. Or looking on in awe at the king of street vendors, my good friend Johnny Kelleher selling newspapers at the Coliseum Corner performing his tantalising tango, ducking and diving between teatime traffic. And etched in my memory is that spiralling sense of teenage urgency as we scrambled from Flower Lodge back into town after a Cork Hibernians game to check the latest League of Ireland results, handwritten by the *Echo* sports reporter Bill George and thumb tacked to the Examiner office door; a quaint and peculiar tradition resonant of Martin Luther nailing his ninety-five theses to the door of Wittenberg church.

But this is not about nostalgia. The clue is in the name – news is now, was then and always shall be all about what is new. And while I wholeheartedly indulge the oddities and eccentricities of the past, I fully embrace new technologies and eagerly anticipate what the future might hold. These days, EchoLive.ie has a fully integrated online presence pumping out breaking news, 24/7, fully confident that all news is local.

Maybe it's because I grew up in a newsagents, but there's something about that tactile engagement with newsprint on paper. My guilty pleasure is a rolled-up *Evening Echo* in my arse pocket as I retreat to some quiet inglenook to sit and sip and read what's happening in the real world.

Inchigeelagh.

Inchigeelagh

And so, the winter of discontent draws to a close, the time has come to shake off the dank cloak of global hibernation. I will emerge from the dark days of social isolation and walk towards the light of a new dawn.

When the bells ring out for VC Day (Victory over Covid) I will not dance barefoot in the streets or splash about in some public fountain. No. When Covid-tide is past, it will be my time for reflection. I look back on 2020 with clarity that hindsight brings. And just as the wild Atlantic salmon risks life and fin to return to the mountain stream where they were spawned, I will answer the call of the wild and go back among my own to that place called home.

I was born and bred on the north bank of the River Lee in the heart of Cork city. Home for me was then, and is now, a spaghetti bowl of streets centring on Three Points Corner, where Coburg Street, Devonshire Street and Leitrim Street melt into one. My family has lived and traded here for generations.

I grew up behind the counter of our small newsagent and grocery shop – first opened by my grandfather Connie Creedon and run by my grandaunt Julia. It was a city outlet for all things dairy, butter, eggs and an in-season selection of garden-fresh vegetables from the home farms of Iveleary/Inchigeelagh and surrounding townlands.

The Inchigeelagh Dairy – the name on the fascia board over our door – was an echo of Cork's colonial past – a throwback to a time when the mighty Butter Exchange in Shandon was the financial powerhouse of the city, and the port of Cork was a hub of trade servicing the furthermost reaches of the Empire, while the name of the home parish stood testament to the homeland of my father's people – Inchigeelagh, also known by the tribal name Iveleary or Uíbh Laoghaire: Land of the O'Learys. And maybe that explains why my father had a disproportionate number of friends from the various septs of the O'Leary clan.

It was a long time ago, but to this day I can still see them leaning on our shop counter, laughing faces and cavorting: the brothers Jimmy and Connie from Drimoleague, Teddy O'Leary, the meat merchant, Tadhg O'Leary from The Cork Arms and, of course, my father's lifelong friend Timmy (Pheg) O'Leary. Timmy (Pheg) travelled the road from Iveleary to Cork with my father when they were both young lads. It was a friendship that no man could pull asunder and remained intact 'til death did them part.

Our small community in the centre of the city had a village-like self-sufficiency, where traders and their families lived above their shops. I have memories of our shop doorbell tinkling as Timmy (Pheg) prised it open with his elbow, and without a hint of irony in his voice, he'd call in to my father,

– I'm going to Cork, Connie. Do you want anything from Cork?

As if Cork was a world away, and the hustle and bustle of city life was some far-off exotic place that just so happened to be located around the corner at the top of our street.

This warren of streets was our world, served by our own teashops, shoemakers, butchers, bakers, fishmongers, furniture makers, undertakers and a string of public houses for when the legs needed a rest or the mind needed exercise – we even had our own theatre, picture house and brewery. To this day, that lingering aroma of fermenting hops and malt belching from

Murphy's stack, blending with the ebb and flow of the River Lee at Carroll's Quay, is locked in the memory of my senses as the defining scent of home. While, above the heads of the merchant paupers and princes, the golden fish on the belfry of St Anne's Shandon looked down on us, casting a knowing eye over our little hamlet, where every lamppost, doorstep and crack in the pavement continues to record a living history so vivid to those of us who know.

My father had a very close, yet loose, sense of kinship. Anyone from west of the Gearagh in Iveleary was likely to be called cousin, although he reserved the title of brother for one man only – his brother John, who continued to trade out of the family business in Inchigeelagh. Though it didn't seem so at the time, the two brothers and their wives lived hectic lives: working round the clock while rearing twelve and fourteen children respectively, yet they somehow managed to find time to be together – always unplanned and impromptu and often ending in a song.

Our neighbourhood in downtown Cork city, as defined by The Inchigeelagh Dairy on Devonshire Street, The Iveleary Bar on Coburg Street and Tadgh O'Leary's, The Cork Arms, further along MacCurtain Street. It was a *Little-Iveleary* in the heart of Cork city – a place where Iveleary exiles would meet. The far counter of our shop, just behind the coal bags, became an unofficial parcel office where priceless packages, such as some mother's homemade brown bread baked on a turf-fired bastible in Iveleary, would be dropped off for collection by a son or daughter living in the city. Urban luxuries, like a swath of fabric from The Munster Arcade, or rural necessities, such as a scythe blade, would be delivered by the next available car heading west. Then, on Friday afternoons, a string of scholars, civil servants and seminarians would gather on the windowsill of our shop, peeling off in ones and twos for the unscheduled yet inevitable lift home.

Iveleary people came to our shop counter for that taste of home – the milk, eggs, butter and cream – but most of all they came to talk. They found comfort in the past, and the past was never some faraway place. It was nothing out of the ordinary to hear the Irish language spoken at our shop counter. It was the language of Iveleary and, regardless of religious persuasion or political conviction, lovers of the native tongue would drop by for an opportunity to joust their eloquence *as Gaeilge*.

They talked of births, deaths and marriages, and the antics of Johnny Jerry's sow, while escapades of guerrilla days were recalled in the hushed tones of a need-to-know basis and the tales of Tim the Tailor and his wife Ansty were always good to fill a gap. Age-old challenge matches between rival townlands were replayed, blow-by-blow, like ancient battles between warring clans, and, of course, there was always that county champion-ship when my father and his brother John lined out for Iveleary. Like gladiators of old, the contest became more epic with each retelling. The words of Patrick Kavanagh beautifully capture the essence of the tales of the townland:

> *'Til Homer's ghost came whispering to my mind.*
> *He said: I made the Iliad from such*
> *A local row. Gods make their own importance.*

The Inchigeelagh Dairy was an outpost of Iveleary here in the heart of Little-Iveleary. Maybe that explains why this boy, born and reared in downtown Cork city, grew up with a sense that home was someplace else. In time, I realised that, for the people of Iveleary, fifty miles may as well be five thousand when you're away from home, and like immigrants who gather anywhere across the globe, home is the birthplace of past generations. Home is always defined as another place in another time.

Let me tell you about Iveleary …

Iveleary is a mysterious and enchanting land where history and story go hand in hand, fact and fiction dovetail seamlessly, and the spiritual and natural complement each other without contradiction or contrivance. This is a world of holy men and holy women – where mystics, monks and hermits have cast their spells and banished evil.

And just as Moses struck the rock of Horeb at Meribah, the source of the River Lee seems to percolate from high up over Gougán and gathers below in a glacial lake at a place once known as Lough Irse. It was here, in the sixth century, at the lake isle oratory of Gougán Barra, that Finbarr drove out the evil Luiwee, a lake monster immortalised in stained glass as a blood-red dragon crushed beneath Finbarr's feet. Luiwee's slithering escape to the sea became the waterway now known as Anna Lee. And so Finbarr is patron saint of these parts. Yet, as if by some supernatural reordering of gender equilibrium, further investigation along the nave reveals another window dedicated to Gobnait.

Gobnait spun her own animal magic when she sent out her squadrons of bees to defend the nearby parish of Ballyvourney. Devotion to this female divinity is still palpable at the old graveyard and abbey. There you will find her miraculous *Iron Ball* concealed within the ancient wall, flanked by Muintir Críodáin standing sentinel. Gobnait's Well was a place of pilgrimage long before the chime of Christianity's bell, and as an echo of that pagan past, a provocative Síle na Gig sensually stretches her thighs high up on the old abbey wall, offering unconditional fertility to all. This is a world where Christian devotion and Pagan belief sit comfortably side by side.

Iveleary holds the secrets of stone circles and megalithic alignments. Bronze Age dolmens span time just as the ancient clapper bridges span the River Lee at Ballingeary. This place of sacred wells and spiritual sites continues to offer comfort and protection to a people who share a collective memory. On the outskirts of Inchigeelagh, a prehistoric *crannóg* on Lough Allua was once a place of sanctuary to a long-forgotten people, yet their blood and sweat have enriched this soil, and the imprint of their footsteps laid the foundations for what is now the scenic South Lake Road.

Like a river of poets and patriots, the history of Iveleary flows in an endless stream of heroes and heroines. The wild and fiery Auliffe O'Leary, who rode with The Great O'Neill and later died during a botched cattle raid at the river crossing of Athakeera. And brave Kedagh O'Leary (*Lieutenant to the King*), who led the men of Iveleary at the head of James II's Jacobite army. Not forgetting the impetuous, vain-glorious Art Ó Laoghaire, immortalised in Eibhlín Dubh's *Caoineadh*. My childhood curiosity was held spellbound by the *seanchaí*-inspired tales of *an tAthair* Peadar O'Laoghaire, and my boyhood imagination ran wild with the swashbuckling escapades of Daniel Florence O'Leary as he rode with Simón Bolívar's liberation army across the plains of South America.

Whenever O'Learys gathered, my father would sing the seditious verses of Máire Bhuí Uí Laoghaire's *Cath Chéim an Fhia*, a tradition now carried on by my cousin Joe. The bravery of the women of Iveleary will be forever remembered for their frontline action standing shoulder to shoulder and breast to bayonet among the Defenders at the bridge of Drom an Ailigh, and the subsequent all-female ambush of the landlord's agent Terry as he and his armed escort rode through Inchigeelagh. We celebrated my grandmother Nora Cotter's family, the Cotters of Currihy, who stood firm with the Defenders, and basked in her connection to the infamous Mother Jones, a labour activist identified as *the most dangerous woman in America*. Her war cry – *Pray for the dead and fight like hell for the living!* – still resounds wherever blue collars assemble.

And so to Fenian times and Pagan O'Leary from Inchigeelagh who inspired generations with the simplicity of his message – *No crown! No collar!* And the quick-witted bravery of young Máire Ní when she secured the escape of a fugitive Fenian, her deed forever celebrated in the local anthem *My Inchigeelagh Lass*. Ever since the dawn of history this rebellious land has offered sanctuary to outlaws who fought the good fight. Not least, General Tom Barry and the boys of his IRA flying columns who led the Black and Tans on a merry dance around the lakes and hills of Iveleary before driving them into the sea and away from our shores, just as Finbarr banished Luiwee.

And so, when the bells of VC Day ring out across the world, I will travel west to Iveleary. It's there you'll find me, happiest among my own in the heart of Inchigeelagh in the company of my cousin Joe Creedon. There we will drink tea.

Maybe it's the stag's head above the fireplace stirring up long-forgotten memories of Máire Bhuí and the Battle of Chéim an Fhia, or the photograph of General Tom Barry sitting proud among the elderly Boys of Kilmichael, or maybe it's that epic photo of our two families – both our parents surrounded by their twenty-six children.

Whatever the reason, there we'll sit and talk, because the time is always right for storytelling in Inchigeelagh. Later, me and my cousin Joe might amble east along the village to the old graveyard. We might stop at an ancient tilting headstone, all trace of etched words wiped clean by time, yet Joe will identify the remains buried beneath the soil as some relative of Art O'Leary. Or he might place his hand on a lichen-encrusted sepulchre and utter the words Maire Bhuí. Every stone tells a story like a benchmark through time itself. Joe will find a moment to remember those who went before, sometimes in a verse of song or a line of poetry. Then we'll return to the fireside for more tea and apple crumble hot out of the oven – the best this side of Kealkill.

The stories will flow and a new generation will learn and know, so at some future date they will step into the shoes that have been worn by many generations before.

The story of Iveleary is a passionate tango of love and war. It sweeps and swirls along the beautiful green and leafy Lee Valley, from its mystical source high up over Gougán and all the way to the broad meandering latticework of waterways of the great southern delta of *Corcach Mór na Mumhan*.

Iveleary is not a destination. Iveleary is a sound, a scent, a state of mind.

A Most Expensive Item
of Clothing

Christmas? A funny time of the year is Christmas. It's enough to put the head spinning and the mind doing somersaults. It's a time when bygones become bygones and those dead and gone are remembered. It's a time when the pain of loneliness finds comfort in candles and fairy lights and the lonesome sound of Shane McGowan singing of fairy-tale nights. It's a time when the rich live like there's no tomorrow, spending what they haven't got – and the poor live like there's no today, spending what they'll never have. Christmas is an island of insanity that carries us through the bleakest of mid-winter with a contrived cornucopia of plenty in anticipation of the first green shoots of spring. Christmas is a time of excess, and maybe that's why I found myself pondering that most revealing question: What is the most expensive item of clothing I have ever bought?

Expensive clothing has never been high in my hierarchy of needs. My circumspect austerity has always been guided by my financial circumstances. But as I pondered my purchasing prowess, it occurred to me that I am seldom in a position to give in to the temptations of excess – yet I do have one peculiar self-indulgent yet practical purchasing practice that has become a personal Yuletide tradition which I hold dear. And what is Christmas if it's not about tradition.

Well, every single Christmas without fail, I go over to McCarthy's on the Coal Quay, drop in to James, a friend of mine since school days, to buy a pair of shoes. From the moment I enter his shop the banter begins. We talk about the year that's been and the year that's about to begin. We recall a funny memory or two and recycle some mishap or adventure from forty years ago or so. We engage in a past that stretches right back into the last century – back to a time when boots and braces and baggy trousers were all the rage. We chat about this and that and nothing at all, and catch up on births, deaths and marriages.

There is comfort in a camaraderie that straddles decades, and as our chatter clatters along gathering apace, James instinctively plucks a pair of size-10 oxblood Doc Marten shoes from the shelf. He removes them from the box, places them in a bag, and usually includes a gift of a tin of polish or a pair of socks. I hand him the money. He pushes a cash discount back into my fist,

— No, no you shouldn't, says I.

But tradition is tradition, so I reluctantly accept his mate rate, because there's no haggling on the Coal Quay when you're an insider trader.

— See you next year, says he.

— All going well, says I.

I walk out onto the street and into the madness of Christmas week.

Off I strike across the flat of the city, weaving in and out between carol singers, shoppers and Christmas-tree hawkers. And there's something about Christmas that guides me to a haven where I can rest my legs and exercise my mind – The Long Valley, The Hi-B, Le Chateau, Counihan's, The Corner House – or one of Benny McCabe's many houses of well-repute. And there, in some quiet inglenook or snug, I call my first of the day, and brimming with childlike anticipation I take one of the shoes from the bag and examine its every detail – from the trademark crinkling sole to the embossed crest and the trim of yellow stitching around the rim.

Maybe it's the memory of that telltale smell of new shoe leather that has been locked in the olfactory creases of my cranium since boyhood? But to this very day I still experience that magical sense of teenage wonderment that I felt when I held my first Doc Marten in my hands all those years ago.

My purchase of one pair of shoes each year could not be described as extravagant or excessive – but my attachment and reluctance to dispose of worn-out shoes might be considered eccentric by some. Over the years I have accumulated many pairs of Airwear, now in various stages of disrepair, and where an untrained eye will see a molehill of red leather, I see a rainbow of colour. Each individual pair distinguishable by a telltale scuffed toecap, a crease in the leather or a signature worn-down heel. And though most have seen better days, there is life in the old Docs still, called into service when required for a specific duty – fit for purpose. There's my Painting Docs, my Hill Walking Docs, my Work Boot Docs, my Lounge-Around-the-House Docs, my Dancing Docs, my Turner's Cross Docs, my Going Out Docs, my Staying Down Docs – and, of course, for those special occasions I have my Good Wear Docs.

That being said, I must admit that I have, on occasion, reached into the wardrobe and randomly plucked out a left and right – and head off into town wearing a pair where each individual shoe had been manufactured in two different millennia.

It's interesting to note that there, in the ocean of oxblood, is one black pair of Doc Marten shoes, bought in 2007, the year of the financial crash. The year Ireland bailed out Europe, the year our political leaders drove us onto the rocks – the year that will forever be remembered as Black Two-Thousand-and-Seven.

But I digress …

As I sit here, pondering the most expensive item of clothing I have ever bought, it crosses my mind that, down through the decades, I have witnessed many changes of currency from L.S.D. to decimalisation – a fiscal journey from the Irish pound to the Irish punt and all the way to the euro. But every step of the way there has always been one constant, one consistency in a world gone mad – my Doc Marten shoes have kept me connected if not rooted to the planet.

And so, year after year I continue to drop into my friend James to purchase the same pair of shoes, and I calculate the accumulated cost of that same pair of shoes has set me back 1,623 euro, 92 cent in new money. All in all, that's a fair price for over forty years of shoe leather and friendship.

If Christmas is a time of tradition, my once-a-year Yuletide chat with James is an observance I hope to embrace for many years to come. It's interesting that with all our aul' guff and banter, me and James never mention shoes. Then again, I guess it's never really about shoes, is it? New shoes or old news – it's just the excuse for this annual get-together of two boys who sat in the same classroom many, many years ago – forty or fifty years ago, or so. It was a long time ago. A time when people were buttoned up. In the days before Velcro.

Christmas Day falls on a Sunday this year – see you on Saturday the 24th, James.

How-zit-goin?

Walking along the street in Clonakilty a few months back, and who did I bump into coming out of a shop only Mick Lynch.

I know Mick for must be close on forty years. Knew him as a teenager in the Arcadia when we first christened him *Mick the Punk*. Over the years we've connected now and again in a – How-zit-goin? sort of way.

You know the way, bump into him every few years and say,
– How-zit-goin?
Well, that sort of thing.

Early 1980s I was in Canada, and Mick was in London, so we didn't see much of each other during that time. But I did catch him with the post-Stump Bernard in the late '80s/early '90s downstairs in Sir Henry's. An absolutely incredible gig in *Sraide Baile*, a mad labyrinth of a venue reimagined as an Irish village of the 1950s including a schoolhouse, cottage, pub and village square.

By the mid-1990s we were both back in Cork and we saw quite a bit of each other. We'd cross paths at gigs and pubs and gatherings, and anytime we'd see each other on the streets we'd cast a nod of recognition to all that went before.

– How-zit-goin?

We worked on a few projects together. He featured in my radio pseudo-soap *Under the Goldie Fish* (RTÉ, 1994–98). And if my mind serves me right, he was the pyrotechnic guy in myself and Pat Kiernan's *Trial of Jesus* (2000) millennium celebration. And so over the past fifteen years we'd bump into each other every now and again and we'd have a bit of,

Mick Lynch – Mean Features at The Arc, Cork. 1979. Photo: Pat Galvin.

— How-zit-goin?

Anyway, there I was a few months ago walking along the street in Clonakilty with Dogeen and who did I bump into coming out of a shop only Mick.

And as usual we fell into the – How-zit-goin?

— How-zit-goin?

— Not too bad. Yerself?

— Plugging away. Yerself?

— Same ol' ding-dong?

— Just bringin de dog for a walk? Yerself?

— Just comin outa the shop.

— You still up in the other place?

— Naw, gone from there. I'm back in the old gaff now.

— Anywhere around here dat serve the dog?

— Loads! says he.

— Have ya time for a pint?

— No, says he. – But …

That's when he told me that he and the band (Stump) had regrouped and had been jamming in the back room of the Clonakilty Hotel for the past week. They were prepping for a mini small-venue tour.

Mick said they were having their last jam session at six o'clock that evening if I'd like to drop by to hear the finished set. I mean, what do you say to that, like? That's an offer you can't refuse. And I didn't refuse.

So, me and Dogeen sat there in the back room of the Clonakilty Hotel in private audience with Stump as they ripped it up. Their full rep. One classic after the next. What can I say,

— Dowcha, Mick, boy! What a class-A day – all the way.

Of course, that afternoon I had no idea that Mick was grievously ill, and within a short time he would be dead. And maybe it was better that I didn't know. Because our parting that day was the way it should have been, the way it always had been in a *See ya around* sort of way. It was honest, unaffected, casual, sincere, uncontrived. A brief *hug* followed by the word,

— Brilliant, Mick! Brilliant!

— See you back in Cork!

— Chalk it down!

And that was the final *How-zit-goin?* I shared with Mick the Punk.

But it has since crossed my mind that there's friendships and there's friendships and there's friendships. It's impossible to quantify or qualify the many degrees of friendship that exist because each and every one is organic, tailor-made and bespoke. There's no handbook to friendship, no template, no Airfix-kit instruction. Measuring friendship is a bit like counting apples and oranges. I guess some friendships are measured in depth, while others are measured in duration. But it amazes me that stopping to say something as simple as,

— How-zit-goin? …

… can be all the gel that's required to seal a lifetime's bond of friendship.

Thanks Mick.

NOTE

I posted this piece on Facebook on 28th November 2015. Mick died eighteen days later, on 15th December 2015. I'm told, when they showed him this post it brought a big ear-to-ear Mick Lynch smile to his face.

The Year Ireland Was Discovered by the Irish

Looking back on it, I guess she was of seafaring Hiberno-Norse extract, if not a daughter of Queen Maebh herself. Out she stepped, hands perched comfortably on her hips. And with a flick of her head she sent tresses of copper-coloured curls cascading down over squared shoulders.

But I digress …

Come with me to the year 2020. It was the summer of our discontent. It was a time when pestilence stalked the land and the world as we knew it stopped spinning.

For the first time in living memory, St Patrick's Day had been cancelled. It was decided that we should flatten the curve rather than cull the herd, so we came together by staying apart. And though counter-intuitive to our natural disposition, as a nation we embraced the notion of socially distant isolation.

Officially we were in lockdown. The fundamental expression of our Irishness, that instinctive impulse to gather in groups and raise a glass in honour of a birth, death or marriage was outlawed. This pandemic had succeeded where the Statutes of Kilkenny, the Penal Laws and eight hundred years of colonial oppression had failed – Irish culture had been derailed.

Inter-county travel was strictly forbidden, as isolated rural communities feared a deluge of city folk would open the floodgates to a tsunami of infection. With all international

The good ship Naomh Ciarán bound for Inisturk.

flights grounded, the sky was cleared of contrails and, overnight, fortress Ireland became an island once again. No sun-kissed selfies on social media. No photos from the *playas* or the *praias*. No cocktails on the Costas. No sand, sea or sangria. And for the first time the word *staycation* entered the lexicon, and we became resigned to the fact that 2020 would be a *backyard summer*.

Then, on 19th June, a glimmer of hope. It was decreed that travel restrictions across the island of Ireland would be lifted. It was as if John Hinde himself had been resurrected from the grave. Picture-perfect postcard photographs began popping up online; snapshots of tourist traps with all the sham-roguery were back in vogue. Jaunting cars, shillelagh sticks, tweed caps and Foxford rugs – the Irish became more Irish than the Irish themselves. The inhabitants of this island reclaimed sovereignty over ground we had long conceded to cash-paying visitors. From Beara to Ballycastle, summer 2020 will forever be remembered as the year Ireland was discovered by the Irish.

And just like every other family in the country, me and my partner Fiona O'Toole checked the oil and water, filled the tank, put the dog in the back seat and set out on a road trip. We were heading for the island of Inishturk off the Mayo coast – the ancestral homeplace of the O'Toole clan. It was from this isle over a hundred years ago that past generations of Fiona's family had departed for the mainland.

Being tourists in our own land was a revelation, and with our sights set firmly on our destination we were content to meander and let the journey be our reward. We spent that first night on the Beara Peninsula. Watching the sun go down on Dursey Sound, feasting al fresco on fresh monkfish tails and brown bread from

Murphy's mobile food kitchen, the finest dining in the land. The next evening we had moved to County Kerry, where we pitched our tent in the shelter of the Iron Age Staigue Fort near Sneem. Bright and early the following morning we boarded a ferry at Tarbert and crossed the River Shannon into County Clare.

Every twist of the road along the western seaboard reveals the most glorious vista that nature can provide, untouched by human hand, from the endless white sand at Kilkee, to the sheer cliffs of Moher. On we went through the Banner, past the colourful hamlets of Kilfenora, Lisdoonvarna and Doolin, to the stunning exposed flora and fauna of the Burren.

In County Galway we paused for a wander around the City of the Tribes, before heading north to Connemara, stopping off along the way at Patrick Pearse's Cottage in Rosmuc, followed by a quick detour into the romantic heartland of *Quiet Man* country eternally associated with Cong and Maam Cross.

That night we bedded down in Leenane on the shores of majestic Killary Fjord. The following morning we crossed into County Mayo, and with time on our hands we took the scenic route through the stunning open expanse of Doolough Valley to Louisburg. At Roonagh pier we boarded the *Naomh Ciarán* and set a course for Inishturk, happy to share the open deck with a herd of sheep.

In truth I was a little apprehensive that Fiona's spiralling expectation regarding encountering past generations might not be matched by reality. But my concerns were unfounded. Inishturk has been an O'Toole stronghold since the twelfth century, and knowledge of family lines is second nature and instinctive among islanders. A simple inquiry on the quayside and immediately a direct line was identified,

— You're related to Packie O'Toole.

So we set off on foot to Packie O'Toole's farmhouse on the far side of the island. And after a separation of more than a century that spanned four generations, Fiona received such a gorgeous, warm welcome from direct descendants of her kinfolk – the clan O'Toole. It was such a joy to hear recollections and vivid memories of her grandfather, Peter O'Toole – a man she had never known. And just like that, Fiona was home among her own. With pandemic restrictions and social-distance etiquette still in place, we met in the open air and stood a few metres apart – yet this was a profound, deep and meaningful – if not emotional – reunion.

Covid guidelines dictated that visitors should not overnight on the island, so, having chatted for the best part of an hour, surrounded by the most awe-inspiring wild and rugged landscape, the time came for us to bid farewell to Fiona's newfound cousins, vowing to return when Covid-tide had passed.

Summer 2020 presents a fascinating case study on what it means to be Irish. A social experiment of national proportion, with all social gatherings restricted to six socially distanced individuals, and the magic food-to-drink ratio rigidly and legally enforced; a limit of ninety-minutes of alcohol consumption for every nine-euro meal consumed. Looking back on that time the restrictive bylaws seem bizarre, and yet we Irish were steadfast and unwavering in our compliance. So, despite the national stereotype of drink-fuelled maudlin singsongs and bawdy brawling, 2020 will go down in history as a summer of sobriety, with an abiding sense that the whole nation was tucked up in bed each night by 9:30pm.

I remember sitting on a bench in Kinvara, sipping coffee from a paper cup, watching the sun set on Galway Bay. I wondered if we had lost a fundamental aspect of our culture to Covid? Had regulations culled our natural ability to mingle, had that illusive entity we call *craic* slipped between the cracks and fallen between the two stools of health and safety?

And that's when it happened …

I would guess she was of seafaring Hiberno-Norse extract, if not a daughter of Queen Maebh herself. Up she stepped at the far side of the square. And with a flick of her head, she sent tresses of copper-coloured curls cascading down over squared shoulders. And she began to sing:

  — If you're Irish come into the paaaaa-rrlour
    There's a welcome there for you.
    If your name is Timothy or Pat …

And just like that we Irish did what we Irish do best. In the face of adversity we instinctively pulled together and entertained each other. An epic singsong took hold and spread across the square faster than Covid in a packed sauna. And in a summer starved of all competitive GAA, it soon developed into an inter-county sing-off featuring *The Fields of Athenry, The Rocky Road to Dublin, Limerick, You're a Lady* and *The Rose of Mooncoin.* I gave my best rendition of *The Banks.* The most spectacular performance came from a young Chinese couple who sang a duet of *Ni Wen Wo Ai* – you could hear a pin drop. And the rousing chorus of the night was reserved for a Lithuanian woman and her family who sang a show-stopping rendition of *Oi Šermukšnio.*

There was magic on the waterfront that night. And, later, we all slept sound and sober, confident in the knowledge that for thousands of years the varied and diverse peoples of this island had faced adversity: famine, war and poverty. This pandemic was but another milestone in our history. There was a sense that it might be a long war and many would perish, but, to paraphrase Terence McSwiney himself, when all is said and done, we would endure and we would be victorious.

Cónal Creedon outside No. 1 Launderette, Devonshire Street, Cork, 1989. Photo: Barry Fitzgerald.

The Accidental Author

New to social media, I found myself hanging out on a platform with a gang of virtual friends. We were talking about this and that and nothing at all. Someone mentioned *Pancho and Lefty Ride Out*.

Now that was a blast from my past. My first book, a collection of short fiction published by the Collins Press over a quarter of a century ago. Someone else asked if I would send on a copy. So I searched the house high up and low down and, odd as it may sound, no book was found. Here's the thing: I'm a pathological book-giver-away-er, and as my condition suggests, I have an overpowering compulsion to give away books that I hold most dear. And so my copy of *Pancho and Lefty Ride Out* had long gone the way of so many of my favourites.

Surfing the virtual world, from time to time I have come upon little snippets of chatter about *Pancho and Lefty Ride Out*. And every now and then I get an enquiry about its availability. I was intrigued by the interest my little book seemed to generate. So I put up a post on my virtual platform looking for a copy with a view to publishing a short print run to mark the twenty-fifth anniversary of the first edition.

What can I say about the kindness of people that has not been said before? First out of the traps offering his own personal copy was John Breen of Waterstone's, followed almost immediately by a copy from Shirley Fehily. Next, my niece Ellen Fayer, and within a week I had accumulated a neat little stack on my bookshelf courtesy of family, friends and the kindness of strangers. My enquiry seemed to have stirred up a wazzies' nest of interest. Photos of *Pancho and Lefty* began to appear on social media from the eight corners of the globe. Paraphernalia and memorabilia connected with the book began popping up online, including a stack of photographs taken back in the day. My friend from that time, Lillian Smith, unearthed a twenty-five-year-old invitation to the book launch at Murphy's brewery. Then, from nowhere, Eddie and Emma of Frameworks sent me a ten-minute film clip featuring the madness that unfolded on the night of the launch – filmed back in the days when a camera was the size of a filing cabinet.

It was the maddest book launch. Then again, back in the last century before health and safety had been invented, book launches and art exhibitions tended to be rowdy and bawdy affairs. Typically, occasions of attempted drunkenness, yahooing, yodelling, followed by a bop in Zoës, chips, cheese and garlic sauce in Luciano's and then back to a decrepit bedsit in some semi-derelict house in the heart of flatland 'til dawn. The launch of *Pancho and Lefty Ride Out* was one of those memorable nights, the details of which I can't seem to remember. But I seem to recollect that Murphy's brewery placed an embargo on book launches soon after that.

Anyway, there I was for the first time in quarter of a century with a dog-eared copy of *Pancho and Lefty Ride Out* in my hands. So tactile, so evocative, everything about it seemed to tell a story: the touch of it, the look of it, the scent of it. But then, in a startling moment of clarity, it occurred to me that the online chatter surrounding that little ninety-eight-paged, short-run, slim volume was not about the book. No. The curiosity it aroused had nothing whatsoever to do with the book, but rather the interest was all about what the book represented: a time, a place, a state of mind. And just like that, I was catapulted right back to the closing decades of the last century.

It was a time before email, internet or personal computers. A time before CD, DVD, iTunes, Spotify or YouTube. A time when the C60 cassette and a Sony Walkman were all you needed to be wired for sound. A time before the invention of the smartphone, when the most intelligent device in my house was the toaster. Put it this way, it was so long ago that way back then salad came in tins, olive oil was sold in pharmacies and used for dropping into your ear, and bottled water was the biggest joke in town. Jesus, and it seems like only yesterday.

Christmas 1985. George Michael. Don't get me started on George Michael. There he was on the telly, frolicking around in the snow, surrounded by a bevy of beauties. Himself and Andrew Ridgeley, the two of them, one as bad as the other, in their designer-cut, over-sized overcoats, with more money than sense. They were somewhere in the Swiss Alps by a log fire, sipping eggnog, port or brandy – on a fucking skiing holiday, if you don't mind. And we over here in Cork perished with the cold, buying Christmas presents in the pound shop and queueing for a living on the dole.

– *Last Christmas I gave you my heart* – me hole!

By the mid-1980s Ireland had been battered by a gale-force recession, and Cork was in the eye of the storm. Now, let's be clear here, I don't hold George Michael responsible for the economic crash, but it was a time of finger-pointing and *whataboutery*. By 1985 half the town was unemployed, the other half redundant. Verolme dockyard had slung its hook and abandoned ship. Our beautiful English Market had burnt down twice, and the plans were to put the space to more profitable use as a multistorey car park. The Monahan Road Motown of Ford and Dunlop had padlocked their gates, never to open again. The dockers clocked out and shouted last call at The Donkey's Ears – and a string of early-morning houses stacked their kegs by the quay wall for the last time. This port town was going down and going down hard. Cork sank.

A whole generation of school-leavers and graduates clawed over each other to get a seat on the next plane, boat, train or Slattery's bus leaving town. We were striking out to start a new life in the squats, kips and bedsits of Brixton, Berlin, Boston and the Bronx. My story was slightly different; living in Newfoundland, Canada since 1979, I found myself swimming against the tide when I returned home to Ireland during the darkest days of the recession.

I was seventeen years old when I first set foot on Canadian soil. Leaving home in the midst of my formative years seemed to imprint a stylised vision of home in my brain. Home for me became like a George Michael video: all happiness and light; a magical place, where the sun always shone, and smiles were shared with everyone you'd meet and greet. It was like living in a musical with the sing-song sound of people talking and nuggets of gold the size of your fist to be plucked up off the street. But memory is an unreliable witness, and without internet or drone footage to offer corroborating evidence, the mind can play games. So, when word reached me that my mother had been fighting a long, hard battle with no cure on the horizon, I came home and stayed – say no more.

I remember walking across Patrick's Bridge that first morning and something had changed. It was a bit like that transition from Bedford Falls to Pottersville in the movie *It's a Wonderful Life*. And though I'm one of the few who have always held the view that Pottersville was a far more fun place to live than Bedford Falls, that was the movies and Cork in the early 1980s was real life.

The ornate lamps along the parapet were damaged, mantels desecrated. That's when I noticed the string of shops and pubs along Merchants Quay all battered and boarded like a mouthful of broken teeth. The glass facade of Mangan's iconic clock shattered. Jesus, downtown was like a war zone. Flagship shops had taken the brunt of a full economic broadside. The premises of long-dead merchant princes – The Queen's Old Castle, Egan's, Burtons and The Munster Arcade – were decrepit and decayed; doors locked, windows blocked and abandoned. The Savoy, The Pavilion, The Palace – these Victorian music halls of delight and art deco cinemas, once bustling and full of life, were now hollow and empty shells. The Cork of my youth that had been indelibly etched in my brain had fallen into terminal decay – and like Oisín's return from Tír na nÓg, I had dismounted from my white steed and was destined to stay.

The city was destitute. The citizenry strapped, trapped in poverty – not only young school-leavers, this was generational deprivation. Whole families – fathers, sons, mothers, daughters – were all unemployed. And it is a sad state of affairs when there was no work for a once-proud working class.

AnCO was the only game in town. Initially established to train apprentices for the trades. But as the recession advanced, the trades receded, and AnCO became less discerning; less about offering realistic employment or career opportunities, and all about keeping the new poor, the redundant aspiring middle classes, failed business owners, nurses, teachers and university graduates off the dole.

My abiding memory of that time was walking the streets with empty pockets looking for diversion. It was a time when turning a bob was a full-time job. And yes – it was a time of bleak bedsit land, damp and draughty flats, skip-scavenging to feed open fires, strumming guitars for entertainment, queues stretching around the block on White Street. Everyone pulling a stroke just to get by. It was a time of whispered passwords through sliding hatches; a time of ten-spots, touts and backhanders; a time when draconian licensing laws saw nightly police raids on semi-legal nightclubs and drinking dens. The frustration could be neatly summed up by Yosser Hughes when he uttered the immortal words – *Gi's a job. I can do that ...*

But don't get me wrong, there was fun to be had back then – but it's a different sort of fun when you've nothing to lose. It's a different kind of tension when law-abiding folk are forced to straddle the black economy. It's a different type of reality when people lose hope. It became a time of subversive activity, and the hard line of legality became blurred at the edges.

Recession and mass unemployment tend to galvanise a population into collective thought, word and deed. Life choices became politically charged – and an angry young population went in search of a banner to stand beneath. I would never consider myself a hard-line activist, but night-time public marches through the streets of Cork became the new going-out. We were marching for peace and marching for war; marching for hunger and marching for hunger strikers; marching for equality and marching for inequality. But above all we were marching for jobs and, in retrospect, we the disenfranchised were marching for any campaign that was denied a voice at the table in this new Ireland.

Every gathering seemed to reach a point where the frontline came face to face with the thin blue line of law and order – and so the chasm between *the haves* and *the have-nots,* between *us* and *them* became more entrenched and polarised. We were the redundant generation that had been cast on the scrapheap, and maybe some of us were unsure of the cause we were rallying around, yet we seemed to find ourselves on the same side of the line as the marginalised voices of inequality, shouting for parity of gender and sexuality, for civil rights and an end to apartheid. It was an era that gave rise to Cork's own Pat the Picket, now sadly departed. And in keeping with the black humour of the time, it was respectfully agreed by those who attended his funeral service that Pat's first action in the afterlife would be to mount a picket at the Pearly Gates.

It was a time of positive action when something as simple as a photocopier in the right hands was considered seditious, a time when resources shared among people doing it for themselves gave rise to iconic keystones of the city, such as the Quay Co-op, the Cork Artists' Collective, Triskel. A time when pubs such as Loafers, The Phoenix and The Spailpín stood for something and by their very existence and tolerance they became resources in themselves.

Having done my time in Canada, I turned my back on the verdant faraway hills of the Great White North, found myself in Cork and decided to stick around. I picked up odd jobs here and there, dabbling in everything from the fringes of pirate radio, to trimming the grass around the headstones at the Quaker graveyard. Eventually, I got on an AnCO start-your-own-business course, a new government initiative to kick-start the economy by enticing people off the live register. The plan was to encourage entrepreneurial spirit with a small cash lump sum paid into the hand, then after that you were on your own, expected to make your way without further government assistance.

I opened my launderette at 1 Devonshire Street in 1986. At the counter of that steam-filled, hot and sweaty, damp and condensation-dripping little shop I met the most interesting spectrum of humanity. Ordinary, everyday people from all walks of life, people who had time to stop and talk, people who had time to think. My launderette became a meeting place for poets, writers, musicians and actors; a meeting place of minds and for those who valued and validated creative expression. My little launderette became a magnet for gatherings. For a while it doubled as a neighbourhood micro brewery, and I would guess it is one of the few launderettes in the world to be raided by the boys in blue during one particularly boisterous poetry reading – our cultural soirée was summarily shut down unceremoniously with threats of arrests. To be totally honest, at times running that launderette was like going to war, but my launderette was my education. And when the Backwater Artists moved into a warren of old warehouses at the bottom of my street, maybe twenty or so artists, a world of creativity opened up before me like Aladdin's Cave. The Backwater Artists represented the generation who, just like me, dug their heels in and stayed.

Ever since I opened the launderette I had been writing frenetically, filling copybook after copybook, putting word after word down on paper, but to no end and with no grand plan. Not so much stories, but observational semi-autobiograph-ical scribbles. Short lyrical vignettes: not poetry as such, but abstractions that seemed to instinctively form a narrative of sorts. Publication was the furthest thing from my mind. I'm not sure any of it was publishable in any commercial sense. But it didn't matter. I was writing for writing's sake and loving it.

Up to that point I had been too shy or too coy to claim ownership or authorship of my words. I was in the habit of having my handwritten manuscripts typed at the Cork Secretarial College around the corner on Patrick's Hill. I would tell a white lie and say that I was dropping off a story that had been written by a *friend*. Over time the staff and students at the college twigged that my imaginary writerly *friend* was actually me. And so it was there in that secretarial college on Patrick's Hill that I found my first readers. Securing an impartial readership, albeit a student in a typing pool, was a big step for me. It paved the way for my first third-party reviews. Comments scribbled by the typist on the return envelope, something as simple as – *I liked this one.* Or – *It was too sad, small Paudie should not have died in the end.*

With my audience of one firmly consolidated and a handful of handwritten third-party reviews under my belt, I submitted to literary festivals. To my surprise the work received recognition and several literary awards.

My story *Come Out Now, Hacker Hanley!* was adapted for radio as part of the P.J. O'Connor Awards and produced by RTÉ 1. This opened a window of opportunity to write for radio, and following a frantic week devising a pilot, I was commissioned to write a ten-episode series. *Under the Goldie Fish* was conceived as a surreal exploration of my neighbourhood and the lives of those who lived in a spaghetti bowl of streets and lanes beneath the golden-fish weathervane of Shandon steeple.

Under the Goldie Fish took off at a gallop and quickly established a hardcore loyal audience who tuned in to this mad, bizarre, daily pseudo-soap with storylines as far-fetched as alien abduction, time travel and a Cork caped crusader Captain Crubeen who could be relied upon to always save the day. The original ten-week series grew legs and ran and ran – extended to a four-year production from 1994 to 1998, eight series and clocking up over four hundred episodes – cited by the *Irish Times* radio critics as Best Radio Programme for 1996 and 1998.

Under the Goldie Fish stands out as a most fantastical, exciting, off-the-wall creative time. It was a seat-of-our-pants production line, at times still editing within minutes of broadcast. It reflected a world where real-life events and people sometimes unfolded as fiction over the airwaves. Surrounded by every actor in the city and working with producer Aidan Stanley and sound engineer Denis Herlihy in his recording studio located in Knapp's Square, just around the corner from my launderette, fun factor became the order of the day. It was during those intense years that I learned that true creativity could only be achieved when fear of ridicule is abandoned.

I moved from scribbling at the counter of my launderette to the relative comfort and privacy of writing in my old clapped-out Volvo parked on the street outside. Without strategy, plan or ambition – I became an accidental author.

And so, for the first time in a quarter of a century, I found myself with a well-thumbed and dog-eared copy of *Pancho and Lefty Ride Out* in my hand. This tactile connection to a very specific time in my past seemed to stir up emotions. I became consumed by memories and personal experiences; some happy, some sad, some downright heartbreaking – some far too personal to reveal here and others so private that my mind is reticent to revisit them at all – and in that split second a vortex of images of decades past flashed in full living colour in front of my eyes.

Maybe it was the curse of a generation lost to emigration, but Cork seemed smaller, more intimate, back then. I remember a chance meeting with Seán Dunne on Academy Street sent me around the corner to Con Collins's bookshop on Carey's Lane. I didn't know Seán, personally or socially. I knew who he was. He was part of the literary elite in the city. At the time, Seán was the books editor with the *Irish Examiner,* and somehow he had come across some of my stories. I believe he may have read some of my stories submitted for the *Irish Examiner*-sponsored Life Extra Short Story Competition – and so I was surprised when he stopped me on Academy Street that day, and as we parted he suggested a publication might be in order.

    – *Tell Con I sent you,* was his personal reference, seal and bond.

Con Collins accepted my bundle of scripts for consideration. On my return to the bookshop a week or two later, Con had a note from the then unknown-to-me at the time Tom McCarthy the poet. Tom had adjudicated the work, and his words of affirmation in broad strokes of penmanship across the A4 clearly stated,

    – *These stories need to be published.*

And so, the publication of my first book was set in progress. Nancy Hawkes worked with the Collins Press at the time and in the intervening years she has gone on to new heights in the world of publishing. It was fortuitous for me that I met Nancy, because so began our freewheeling friendship that has spanned over a quarter of a century and continues to grow in strength and depth.

Now, maybe I should make it clear that I'm not in the habit of reading my own books. But as I stood there with this twenty-five-year-old time capsule in my hand, I succumbed to the overpowering desire to bend back the spine and flutter through the pages.

Aware that this little book had originally been written longhand, it struck me that by today's technological standards the transfer of text from biro-marked page to printer's block offered limited opportunity for correction. It had been published in the pre-digital world, a time when computerised word processing was still in its infancy. So, at first glance, I saw the flaws. The work needed a cold editorial eye and a well-honed scalpel – but all that aside, my eyes couldn't resist the urge to read on.

What surprised me most of all was how personally revealing the writing was. The narratives explored and characters exposed seemed to present pure autobiography thinly veiled as fiction. It dawned on me that maybe my initial obsessional struggle with the page may have been a homespun self-therapy of sorts. It then became apparent that these seminal extracts and unfinished fictions were in fact, unbeknownst to me at the time, works-in-progress of future published texts.

The two stories with Limbo in the title are clearly early drafts of what eventually became my novel *Passion Play*. An amalgamation of *He Ain't Heavy* and *The Entomologist* seemed to dovetail together as an early draft of my stage play *The Cure*. *Same Old Tune* presents a serious, non-comedic exploration of my comic character Nero, who featured large in *Under the Goldie Fish*. *Arthur, the Exhibitionist and Nigel Rolfe* is clearly a lament for the demise of the short-lived boot-boy era of my teens, later explored in more detail in *Passion Play* – the narrative also presents a record of the development of Triskel Arts Centre from a single-roomed basement on Bridge Street to the arts centre it became on Tobin Street. I was surprised to find that I had name-checked Robbie McDonald. Though not blatantly obvious, *Every Picture Tells a Story* is most certainly inspired by aspects of the *Cork Art Now* exhibition hosted by the Crawford Gallery during the late 1980s – and is a veiled homage to artist James Scanlon who had given me a painting that still to this day hangs in my front room, simply signed Scan '94. Even the inclusion of a number of references to pigeons offered insight into a theme I would revisit in my work many years later – in my documentary *The Boys of Fair Hill*, my *Irish Times* column 'Video Paradiso' and, of course, most significantly in my novel *Begotten Not Made* in the character Dowcha Boy. And yet, with all this fiction-in-progress I was most perturbed by the sheer amount of personal soul-searching and autobiography laid bare, invisible to the unsuspecting eye, but jumping out at me from each and every page. *Penny for Your Thoughts* is probably the most flawed piece in the collection and yet for me it stands as one of the more revealing and interesting.

It occurred to me that rereading *Pancho and Lefty Ride Out* was far more than a sentimental journey of nostalgia. This little book presented a serious reassessment of my own personal past, and I was surprised by what I found. I decided there and then to let sleeping dogs lie. I thought it best to rebury the time capsule that is *Pancho and Lefty Ride Out*. Fortunately, over the decades, most of the stories in *Pancho and Lefty Ride Out* have been re-edited, republished and transferred to digital format for inclusion in various anthologies. Others had been reimagined and adapted as radio plays, stage plays and monologues.

And so, for those with a passing interest in reading *Pancho and Lefty Ride Out*, I decided to collect together the digitally remastered versions with additional bonus tracks to mark the twenty-fifth anniversary of its publication with a new revised edition *Pancho and Lefty Ride Again*.

George Michael? Ah, me and George made our peace a long time ago. He was just another lad like me, trying to make his way in bleak times. He was living the dream, giving those of us who had stopped believing in fairy tales some idea of what a dream might be – Dowcha, George! As I say, it took time, but in time I learned to – *Listen Without Prejudice*.

The launderette? Well, suffice to say my obsession gradually became my occupation, and after a dozen years or so washing clothes, I set the spin cycle one last time – then shut my launderette down. Or more to the point, one day I just didn't open the door. For many years it remained there silent, undisturbed and intact like Miss Havisham's wedding table.

And the rest, as they say, is fiction …

Café Culture

I was recently commissioned by the Shanghai Writers' Association and the *Shanghai Daily* newspaper to write about the current global wave of coffee culture. But before I begin my exploration of Western literary café culture in the context of a Chinese teahouse culture, I would like to share two anecdotal stories related to Irish pub culture in China.

China is the tea basket of the world – and so the age-old sage advice against bringing tea to China is well founded. Well, fifteen years ago, during one of my first visits to Shanghai, I found myself in an Irish bar in Puxi. It was late into the night, a *lock-in* situation, just me and the owner, an ex-pat Irishman. We were talking about this and that and nothing at all. It had become apparent to him that I hailed from Cork city – and at a certain point in the night, having mutually gained each other's confidence, I was invited into the back room behind the bar. Reminiscent of a scene from Rick's Bar in *Casablanca*, there in the corner stood a strong box about the size of a small wardrobe.

– You'll appreciate this, he said, as he took a bunch of keys from his pocket and proceeded to unlock the safe. – You'll never guess what I have in here …

I expected to see contraband of some sort. Or maybe gold ingots or cash. At the time, cash was king in China, especially foreign currency. So it crossed my mind that I would see stacks of foreign exchange: sterling, dollars and euro …

But when the heavy, iron-clad door swung open, I was surprised that not even as much as an Albanian lek was to be seen. And there in the backroom of that bar in old Shanghai, my cranium contorted as my brain struggled to make sense of what my bulging eyes did see.

There, stacked solid, jam-packed, crammed from back to front and locked away in the highest security of lock and key, he had stored boxes of Barry's tea and Tayto.

    – This is solid gold out here, he said. – But d'ya know what? You can't get Tanora for love or money …

The lesson I learned that night was: there's no point bringing tea to China unless, of course, it's Barry's best.

My second anecdotal tale relates to the opening of the first Irish pub in Shanghai.

Anyone who knows anything about Irish pubs will agree that pub culture is not necessarily all about drink. It's a culture so deeply ingrained in the Irish psyche that it's difficult to define. It's not about music, dance, song, conversation, births, deaths and marriages. It's not about politics or religion. It's not about sport. And yet it's about all those things. Irish pub culture is elusive – and just when you think you have the essence of what makes a good Irish pub, it's gone. It evaporates in front of your eyes and that probably explains that sinking feeling when you find yourself at the counter of an *Irish pub* in some far-flung foreign land. You're sitting there with a pint of Beamish in your hand, the lingering aroma of turf smoke wafting from the nebuliser, the sound of diddle-e-eye, the obligatory poster of Dublin writers or Dublin Georgian doors framed in some shrine, altar or alcove, and a mass-produced *stolen* road sign with *INCH 1 Mile* on the front and *Made in China* on the back. And a plethora of wise and witty Irish sayings hanging from every hook, nail and picture rail. You find yourself sitting there drowning in a sea of familiarity.

The Irish pub, a bit like the Chinese restaurant, has become a global phenomenon. No matter what town, village or crossroad you ride into – be it in the most remote corner of the globe – as sure as the publican's name up over the door is Shannon O'Finnegan, there you'll find the Irish pub, flying the flag for Irish culture.

They say that if you can remember the night the first Irish pub opened in China you probably weren't there. It was sometime back in the mid-'90s. Word had been filtering through from the fourth estate that something big was happening on the far side of the planet. And so the frenzy began.

For weeks the Irish national press and our national broadcaster had been highlighting the significance of such a massive international cultural exchange. And so, on the appointed day, China was besieged by Irish culture vultures.

Half the Irish parliament turned up for the pouring of the first pint in China: the Taoiseach, former Taoisigh, cabinet ministers, opposition leaders, senators, high-ranking Irish military personnel with more brocade than Hickey's Homeware curtain department dangling from epaulettes; musicians, story-tellers, set dancers, songwriters, painters, playwrights, poets and poseurs. You had your hurlers and soccer players and a scrum of rugby prop forwards holding up the bar. The place was chock-a-block with council junketeers, civil servants, town planners, arts administrators, funding bodies and quangos. I think I was there myself – reading a story about some aul' fella who had built his own coffin in the kitchen at home.

My abiding memory of the evening was the chorus line of *Riverdance* leading the Taoiseach in a few high kicks on *'The Walls of Limerick'* (or was it *'The Bridge of Athlone'*?) down the Nanjing Lu. And before we called it a night, it was time to go someplace else …

Ah yes, one of those nights. The place was in full tilt, heaving, bursting at the seams – drink pouring and flowing left, right and centre. Six competing sing-songs, tap dancing on tabletops, and every so often a rousing chorus of *'The Fields of Athenry'*. There was even a lad from Roscommon there – he impressed all assembled with his ability to drink a full pint of stout from a glass in one go while standing on his head – I jest you not.

And it crossed my mind – how wonderful it was that we Irish celebrated the opening of the first Irish pub in China, but could you imagine if this carry-on happened every time a Chinese restaurant opened in Ireland …

Ah yes, Culture – with a capital *C* – is all about perspective.

*

And so, to my exploration of Western literary café society in the context of Chinese teahouse culture.

Café culture – particularly in a literary sense – is relatively new to Ireland. Traditionally, every milestone of Irish life – be it birth, death or marriage – has been benchmarked by a visit to a public house, more commonly known as a pub. It's true to say that certain similarities exist between the Chinese teahouse and the Irish public house. Though the Irish may not exercise the same reverence when pouring a pint as the Chinese attach to the centuries-old tea-making ceremony – yet seasoned Irish-stout drinkers will insist it takes exactly 119.5 seconds to pour the perfect pint – not a half second less or a half second more.

Here in Ireland, pub culture is as nuanced and layered and complex as life itself, ranging from the elite cocktail bar frequented by the glitterati and the upper echelons of society to the downbeat drinking den of the literati hoi polloi – there, where rents are low, is where you will find the Irish literary scene. Writers, actors, artists and musicians tend to congregate at the dark end of the street, on the wrong side of town, in establishments where the chaos of creativity is not only tolerated but welcomed and often encouraged.

These bastions of bohemian boisterous bawdiness offer safe haven for young creatives to think and express without censure in a fertile gene pool of ideas and anarchic thought. This is a world where the artistic connect with the altruistic, the vagabond and the vainglorious rub shoulders, and the egotist and eccentric see eye to eye in a simmering hotpot of low-life high jinks and aspirational ambition.

Irish writers seldom write in pubs – some would say it might be considered pretentious. Personally, I'm from the school of thought that says write where you can. My early creative years were spent writing longhand in my old clapped-out car outside my launderette in downtown Cork city. These days the sweet solitude of writing at a desk at home seems far more conducive to the act of processing creative thought. Similarly, the thought of a *literary salon* of writers gathered at some bar counter discussing high art and imparting nuggets of insightful cultural wisdom is fanciful and notional to say the least.

Of course, the Irish pub is not devoid of artistic discourse or literary discussion. The inglenook of ale houses the length and breadth of the country have long been a forum for heated debate. This is where book clubs meet to deconstruct, reconstruct and analyse. Meanwhile, arts events and literary festivals are very much an integral part of Irish pub life.

My home city of Cork in Ireland has a vibrant arts scene, with numerous pubs renowned as meeting places for writers, musicians and artists. Typically, these establishments are dimly lit, festooned with quiet alcoves, corners, nooks and crannies – the sort of place where people go when the legs need a rest, and the mind needs exercise – the sort of place where people can sit and talk at ease in comfort and without interruption.

In recent decades the rise of tourism, and in particular the popularity of what has become known as the *city break*, has made it financially expedient for various cities across the globe to identify, celebrate and exploit their literary and artistic heritage. Tourist maps in hotel foyers offer an *insider's* guide to every snug and stool that has graced the arse of some alcohol-swilling scribe – witty quotes and anecdotes abound, and portraits adorn the walls.

All tourist maps lead to tourist traps – consequently, the current crop of creatives will have long fled the scene and moved to pastures green before anyone realises they had been there in the first place. The life expectancy of any specific artistic or literary scene is short, often falling victim to its own success – enticing the unwanted attention of investors, paving the way for gentrification and the crushing ball of development. Alas, all that remains of the heady glory days of free-thinking debauchery is an empty shell, like a sanitised museum piece of what once was. So, if you expect to sip a Scotch with Dorothy Parker at the Algonquin in New York or hope to find Hemmingway holding court at Le Deux Magots in Paris or intend to joust words with Joyce at Davy Byrne's in Dublin – you will be disappointed.

The resurrection of long-dead cultural haunts to entice tourists and satisfy the whim of marketeers has become a global trend. The famous Wolff et Beranget Confectionery in Saint Petersburg, Russia, is now conveniently renamed the Literaturnoe Kafe (the Literary Café) and celebrates its heritage with a wax effigy of the poet Aleksander Pushkin sitting at a table by the window. In Buenos Aires, Argentina, the Café Tortoni boasts a gathering of life-sized poetic legends Jorge Luís Borges and Alfonsina Storni with singer and tango aficionado Carlos Gardel. Meanwhile, the three-hundred-year-old George Inn in London has had a phoenix-like rebirth since it was reimagined as a literary pub. Built in 1698, the original George Inn was destroyed by fire on a number of occasions. It was later rebuilt and repurposed as an annex to Guy's Hospital. Then it served as a storage depot for the Great Northern Railway, before being partially demolished during redevelopment of the railway network. Finally, unrecognisable from the original building, it was taken over by the British National Trust in 1937, which salvaged what remained of the site. Archival research led to copper-fastening literary connections to Shakespeare and Dickens. The George Inn has now become a must-visit on the tourist literary trail of London, but one wonders if the literati discovered The George Inn, or could it be the case that The George Inn discovered the literati.

Back in 2007 I was invited as a guest of the Shanghai Writers' Association to take up a literary residency in the city. It was my introduction to China and proved to be a life-changing experience. It was as if Shanghai and its people had cast a spell on me, like I was enchanted by the sights, sounds and scents of this Pearl of the Orient. And so I have returned to Shanghai many times over the years to present readings, screenings of my documentaries, and productions of my stage plays.

On my first visit to Shanghai I was fascinated by the vast number of teahouses in the city. But then again, that's not surprising, China is the tea basket of the world, a tradition said to stretch back five thousand years all the way to the mythological emperor Shennong, in 2737BCE.

I have so many fond memories of visiting teahouses during my time in Shanghai. But without doubt my most abiding memories are of the literary gatherings hosted by my friends Wang Anyi and Hu Peihua at the offices of the Shanghai Writers' Association on Julu Lu. I was always greeted by the open arms of a genuine Chinese welcome, and I really can't think of a more magnificent location to host a literary gathering.

This building is home to the beating heart of the Shanghai literary scene, with a history steeped in the real-life love story of the original owners, Liu Jisheng and his wife Chen Dingzhen. A love story immortalised in their garden design inspired by the ancient classical mythical romance of Eros and Psyche. As a token of his love for his wife, Liu Jisheng commissioned a statue of Psyche. It was erected as a centrepiece in this green and leafy garden. Alas, during the Cultural Revolution it became prudent to divest of such blatant Western imagery. And so the statue disappeared, and its very existence was soon forgotten.

But many years later the former gardener visited the house, and by chance he mentioned that he had removed and buried the statue in the garden for safekeeping. This came as a surprise to the new residents of the building. The effigy of Psyche was duly exhumed from the soil and reinstated to pride of place on display as a centrepiece in the garden where it had been originally located – on Julu Lu. Incidentally, the image of Psyche is now the iconic logo of the Shanghai Writers' Association.

Literary culture and café culture seem to fit together seamlessly in Shanghai. The renowned modernist left-wing writers who frequented the tea houses around Duolun Road in Hongkou District back in the 1930s have left their indelible mark on the literary landscape and history of the city. And though the nature of any literary scene is transient, culture will always survive and thrive, and continues to flow through Shanghai like the mighty Huangpu River herself.

An unprecedented surge in coffee consumption across the globe in recent decades has caused a subtle but sustained move away from the teahouse and public house. It's as if every city across the planet has been hit by a caffeine tsunami. It is difficult to identify precisely where, when or why this phenomenon began, but it most definitely was spearheaded by the arrival onto the world stage of the multinational coffee-roaster giants such as Starbucks. And like so many others of my generation, who initially resisted the allure of the freshly ground coffee aroma, the seductive hissing of steam from the coffee machine, the slick customer service and the cool swagger of the baristas, I was slow to embrace this new wave of *coffee-to-go* in a paper-cup culture – but even King Canute himself could not have turned the tide of this global coffee revolution.

On mature reflection I now realise that this cultural shift was not the result of some Machiavellian marketing ploy – it seems that serendipity had a hand to play. Thanks to the spiralling popularity of the personal laptop computer, the writer is no longer chained to a desk. The writer's desk is now mobile and fits neatly into a shoulder satchel. It seems the meeting of wi-fi on the move and coffee-to-go became the perfect marriage between culture, commerce and technology. And when the literary giant J.K. Rowling endorsed The Elephant House café in Edinburgh as a location where she wrote, it opened the gates to a new era of café culture, where young writers in a café, staring at a laptop screen, fingers tapping on a keyboard, became de rigueur.

During a recent visit to Shanghai I witnessed the future of

café culture, a phenomenon that has become known as the *book café* – book cafés such as The Mix Place, ZiWu and Sinan Books, where the emphasis is on readers rather than writers. With books stacked to the ceilings, readers are invited to come and linger and read while sipping a caffeine hit of choice. Truthfully, I'm not sure such a business model and sales strategy would catch on here in the West, where the *turn-a-buck* strategy of *get them in, get them out* seems to prevail. But hey? What do I know?

Maybe I'm just old school or too long in the tooth, maybe I just like the bohemian bawdiness of a pub in full flight, or maybe I just like the simple sound of a pen scratching on paper. For me, writing will always be my endeavour to engage with the page, my pursuit of splendid solitude to find that place where the internal monologue of fiction can live and breathe and dance and sing inside my soul, unhindered by the social niceties or the expectations of reality. On the other hand, the public house is that magical mystical place where I go to engage with the wild imaginings of reality itself.

The Boys of Fairhill

When I stand on St Patrick's Bridge and look northwards to the Red City of Gurranabraher, I can identify the owners of the various flocks of pigeons flying above the city. My twelve-year-old niece insists it's a superpower. I'm not convinced. I see it as an extraordinary gift I acquired in the company of exceptional people during the magical summer of 2007.

I have always been fascinated by the superpowers of Na Fianna. The ancient manuscript Agallamh na Seanórach (*c*.1200) tells of the final and brutal Battle of Gabhra (AD284), where Fionn mac Cumhaill was slain as he mourned the death of his grandson Oscar. The sole survivors of Na Fianna, Oscar's father Oisín and Caílte Mac Rónáin, lived to tell the tale. Caílte, with his superpower of eloquence, spun a most colourful tapestry of tightly woven lyrics into an Irish epic to rival the *Iliad*. He conjured up the adventures of Fionn mac Cumhaill and his dogs Bran and Sceólang, and how Setanta became Cú Chulainn with only a hurley and *sliotar* to defend himself. Caílte entranced his audience with fantastical tales of Tír na nÓg, the Salmon of Knowledge, the *Táin* bull. And so the story of Na Fianna and their mystical affinity with their animals lives on to the present day.

Ever since our ancestors became aware of their mortality, the search for immortality became an obsession. They lived in the belief that life after death could be achieved for as long as the name of the deceased continued to be spoken. And maybe that's why the oral tradition of the bard and the *seanchaí* is held in such high regard – because through the words of the storyteller the legend lives on.

The Northside of Cork city has a proud culture that permeates every facet of life. This ancient heritage is not preserved intact like a museum piece, but rather a living tradition that continues to evolve right to the present day. It is our song, our story, our sport and the language that we speak. Of course, food is a fundamental expression of all cultural heritage. And here on the Northside our cuisine is legendary – recipes handed down through the generations for local delicacies such as bodice, pig's head, brawn, pressed tongue, crubeens, skirts and kidneys, tripe and drisheen, stuffed heart and more variations on the humble potato than you could shake a stick at.

Fairhill is the backbone of the Northside. Having spent my formative years in the North Monastery, a Christian Brothers' school perched on Fairhill, I had always been aware of its cultural significance.

One bright May morning in 2007 I called to my friend John O'Shea, a singer, a storyteller, a modern-day bard. We were in his shed chatting about this and that when I noticed an old photograph; fifty or so men assembled on the steps of the North Monastery.

— That's the Boys of Fairhill, he said.

John took the photograph from the wall and dusted it with his elbow. Then, one by one, he introduced every man by name: Connie Doyle, Johnny Clifford, Timmy Delaney … identifying each individual in the photograph by their specific sporting prowess: bowler, harrier, pigeon fancier, hurler.

This was John O'Shea at his very best – in full flight, animated and engaging, shuffling stories and characters, dovetailing fact and fiction, presenting anecdotal credibility with an appropriate

The Boys of Fairhill.

verse from Seán O'Callaghan's vast repertoire of songs. John continually reminded me that the only reason Fairhill is immortalised is because of Seán O'Callaghan's songs.

As morning stretched to afternoon, it occurred to me that, just as John O'Shea had been inspired by Seán O'Callaghan's lyrics of past glory, the time had come to pass on the smouldering embers of history to a new generation. And so, over the next few months, John invited me to join him on a most incredible life-reaffirming odyssey into the beating heart of the Northside of Cork city.

Next morning we called to Frank Quinlan, the most celebrated huntsman on the Northside. An invitation was duly extended to visit the Fairhill Harrier Club. It was a special privilege to sit in the company of hounds and their handlers in this ambient clubhouse steeped in history. An Aladdin's Cave of trophies, photographs and taxidermy. The talk was of dogs and demigod dog trainers, such as the great Connie Doyle. In Fairhill lore, no dog will ever equal Ringwood. Such was Ringwood's unbeatable determination that their arch-rivals, the Southern Harrier Club, nicknamed the hound 'The Armoured Car', a hound now immortalised in the words of Seán O'Callaghan's song of the same name.

Facts to you I'll disclose,
he had a checkproof nose,
and he never yet lost a hunt.
He had cast-iron jaws
and steel-padded paws,
every nail was like an iron bar.
From one mile to ten,
he would never give in,
if you ran him from here to Castlebar.
Small wonder, gentlemen,
that the Boys of Fairhill used to call him the Armoured Car.
('The Armoured Car' by Seán O'Callaghan)

I have such special memories of my time with the Fairhill Harriers, striding the undergrowth of Carraig na Bhfear woods, calling the baying pack to heel to the sound of the huntsman's horn. But nothing could have prepared me for the thrill of my first drag hunt. Standing on a hillside, surveying the surrounding country as far as the eye can see to infinity. The sheer exhilaration to witness as many as one hundred hounds released. Running hell for leather over walls and ditches, across ten miles of open countryside, tracking their progress until they are mere dots on the landscape, and then the loop – and they return full tilt back to the very spot on the hillside from where they set out. Magical. It defies description.

The following Wednesday afternoon, I arranged to meet the bowlers down the Blarney Road. And there's something primordial, honest and authentic about a score of bowls. When a bowler is airborne and a twenty-eight-ounce ball of iron is lofted at 70mph, then splits the sop, knocking sparks off stones and comes thundering down the road – it is a sight to behold. Later that day, Denis McGarry, in his own bardic way, regaled us with a blow-by-blow account of the legendary score between Timmy Delaney and Hammerman Donnelly that took place back in 1928.

Of course, hurling and camogie are synonymous with Fairhill. We regrouped at Na Piarsaigh Hurling Club to watch the Munster final on the telly. It was there, in the company of local male and female sporting legends, that I first heard about the ill-fated Fairhill Hurling Club. By all accounts the club disbanded in 1920 after a crushing defeat; beaten by fifteen goals. It's remembered locally as the *Goal-a-Man Final*. Devastated in defeat, it is said they burnt their hurleys after the game. In their defence it was mentioned in hushed tones that their key players weren't available to play that day; caught up in the War of Independence, on the run with the IRA.

But for me the pigeon-racing fraternity stole my heart. Sometimes misunderstood but, nonetheless, a profound culture with a language and tradition all its own. Breeding homing pigeons must be the most highly refined collaboration between human and wild animal. There is something philosophical about pigeon fanciers – I have such happy memories of the days spent with Michael Crane in his loft. Through his passion for the sport I learned to appreciate the regal majesty of pigeons – to witness the flash of iridescent neck plumage as a flock of pigeons bank into the sun is nothing short of mesmerising. A personal high point for me was recently when the current Bard of Fairhill – Denis Twohig – arranged for me to visit Scott Lee's loft on Fairhill, where they named a pigeon *Dowcha Boy* after the fictional Fairhill pigeon who graced the pages of my novel *Begotten Not Made*. Incidentally, my niece Asha accompanied me, and Scott Lee kindly named a recently hatched chick – *Asha* – after my niece.

So that's the way the summer of 2007 unfolded. In the company of pigeons, bowlers, hurlers and harriers.

It struck me that just as Caílte mac Rónáin immortalised the epic deeds of Na Fianna, the Boys of Fairhill will forever be remembered in the songs of Seán O'Callaghan.

In an oral tradition the storyteller becomes as important as the stories they tell. And so to the new generation of bards and balladeers: John Spillane, Jimmy Crowley, Seán Ó Sé, Myles Gaffney, Tim Riordan, Denis Twohig, Marion Wyatt – the story lives on.

Sadly, some of those who so kindly invited me into their lives and welcomed me into their homes and their lofts back in 2007 are now no longer with us. If, as our ancestors believed, life after death can be achieved for as long as the name of the deceased continued to be spoken, so I will whisper the names: John O'Shea, Denis McGarry, Magic O'Callaghan, Jim McKeon.

And so the legend lives on.

Eurovision the Zeitgeist Barometer

To dismiss Eurovision as trite would be an error of judgement – it is a snapshot of what it means to be European at any given moment in time.

Anyone with even a passing interest in Eurovision will have come across Will Ferrell's *The Story of Fire Saga* on Netflix. In a narrative fuelled by an obsession for the Icelandic nonsense lyric *Jaja Ding Dong*, the Eurovision Song Contest is exposed as a cliché-ridden parody of itself – a frivolous, evanescent, inconsequential popular music feast of glitz, glam and glitter. But despite the perceived frivolity, Eurovision has always had its finger firmly pressed to the pulse of the raw, throbbing underbelly of the greater European project. History regularly reminds us that Europe has long been at war with itself, arguably the most violent and volatile piece of real estate on the planet. Staunch allies have slit each other's throats, treaties of peace have been treacherously broken, and the soil has been soiled by the entrails of successive generations – cities levelled and rebuilt, walls constructed and knocked down again, and borders drawn and redrawn across the map in blood-red ink. For millennia the most powerful armies of the world have faced each other across some farmer's field in a wet and boggy lowland to do battle for ground of such low yield it would keep neither snipe nor grouse. Yet, battle-hardened, they stood their ground and fought to the bitter end of total annihilation.

When Julius Caesar stepped out onto the steps of Rome in 58BCE and uttered the immortal words *Omnia gallia in tres partes divisa est,* he identified the kernel of the problem. In his *Commentarii de Bello Gallico,* Caesar explains that the component territories of Europe *differ from each other substantially, in language, customs and laws.*

With an eye to economic growth, Caesar set about a programme of unification through the crude mechanism of the Gallic Wars. To his credit, Pax Romani, which lasted almost 500 years, was probably the most successful attempted unification of Europe to date.

The union remained relatively intact until the Kingdom of Soissons, that contentious piece of ground between the rivers Somme and Seine, fell to the Franks in AD486. From that day to this, reunification has been a work in progress, and the pockmarked fields of Flanders have become the blood clot of Europe, a weeping, seeping scab that is regularly picked raw by attempts at forced unity.

Many have set eyes on this elusive prize, and ultimately all have failed – Hannibal, Attila the Hun and Napoleon, to name but a few. And when Queen Victoria of the House of Hanover married her cousin Albert of the Saxe Coburg-Gotha dynasty in 1840, Europe almost became unified beneath the crown and sceptre of an uber Royal Family. Historians speculate, and most agree, that Pax Victoria might have succeeded had it not been plagued by internal squabbles in Victoria's nursery between the cousins – king, tzar and kaiser.

Alas, we are all too familiar with the most recent brutal and catastrophic attempt to unite Europe around the rallying call of *'One People. One Realm. One Leader'.* The outcome was as divisive as it was tragic, and once again we buried ours and they buried theirs, and the red poppies raised their heads and danced a fandango across the green fields of France.

This never-ending cycle of bloodletting, death, gore and destruction exposed the futility of employing warfare as a unifying force. Maybe that's why, in the aftermath of the Second World War, Winston Churchill came up with the inspired and challenging concept of unity by consent and called for the formation of the Council of Europe.

This paved the way for a convening of the Union of European Federalists. The ensuing isolationism and polarisation of the Cold War seemed to galvanise the formation of the European Economic Community (EEC), which eventually became the European Union (EU).

So why the history lesson? Well, this is the genesis of Eurovision – a love child born into a maelstrom of pan-European projects aimed at healing millennia of hurt. And so, inspired by the Italian Festival di Sanremo, Concours Eurovision de la Chanson was first held in 1956.

Europe of the 1960s would be unrecognisable today. Not a lot had changed since Caesar's observations of 58BCE. From an Irish perspective, perched out here on the western isles off the north Atlantic coast, *The Continent*, as it was known then, was a faraway and exotic place, populated by distinct and sovereign nations, separated by incompatible language, culture and currency.

Back in those days before package holidays, continental travel was an obstacle course of border posts, passport control and visa restrictions, not to mention the required bulging wallet of foreign exchange: franc, lat, guilder, escudo, lira, peseta, Deutschmark and drachma – further complicated by localised fluctuating exchange rates.

It was precisely this regional diversity that gave rise to the often-parodied Eurovision nonsense lyric, such as the now-iconic La-La-La that sealed victory for Spain in 1968, followed by *Boom Bang-a-Bang* for the UK in 1969. This gobbledegook seemed to bridge the chasm between competing cultures hungry to communicate with each other – or at least clap along and join in the chorus. For the first time in our history, Eurovision had the disparate nations of Europe singing from the same hymn sheet in a gibberish we all instinctively understood.

Despite commitment to a strict apolitical code, Eurovision is a blatant flag-waving extravaganza of nationalist triumphalism. But because the winners are selected by a democratic public vote, it has become a highly charged and invaluable platform for dissent. In 2022 the tsunami of public support for war-torn Ukraine's winning entry sent out a clear and undeniable statement from the combined peoples of Europe.

Likewise, in 1969, when Northern Ireland became consumed by spiralling sectarian violence, with thousands of Catholic refugees fleeing south of the border to the Republic and the deployment of British troops onto the streets, it spoke volumes when Dana, a young Catholic schoolgirl from Derry, chose to represent the South of Ireland in the 1970 Eurovision.

Her simple song of hope rose up from behind the barricades, cutting clean through the rhetoric, sabre-rattling and bloody racket of conflict. It was Ireland's first victory in Europe. Within a year, Irish affairs had moved centre stage into the spotlight of European international politics when the Treaty of Accession was signed.

For a more overt expression of Eurovision sedition, one need look no further than the 1974 Carnation Revolution in Portugal. Paulo de Carvalho's Eurovision song was used as the secret signal to overthrow the authoritarian Estado Novo Regime. And right on cue, at 10:55pm sharp on 24th April, when the opening bars were broadcast on Emissores Associados de Lisboa, the revolution began. Democracy was established and the rest, as they say, is history.

Ironically, that same year Swedish pop sensation Abba won the Eurovision with a song celebrating the defeat of Napoleon at Waterloo. And maybe all is fair in love and war. That might explain why, at the height of the South Lebanon conflict of 1978, Jordanian media decided to ignore the existence of the state of Israel when they blocked the live Eurovision performance of Abanabi, the Israeli entry, and simply broadcast that runners-up Belgium had won.

Meanwhile, back where it all began, at the pit face of the Cold War. In 1989 the Western world jumped with joy when Mikhail Gorbachev's policy of glasnost heralded the dismantling of the Berlin Wall. It signalled a rapid expansion eastward that opened the floodgates, releasing a deluge of Eastern Euro-techno-pop that has become so synonymous with Eurovision.

In recent years, contestants have taken a unilateral stand and seized the opportunity to address social issues. In 2009 Dutch semi-finalists The Toppers threatened to pull out of the contest in Moscow if authorities cracked down on a gay pride march. Protesters took to the streets highlighting Russia's poor record on gay rights. Riots and arrests ensued, and the Moscow Eurovision copper-fastened the song contest as a platform to promote the LGBTQ+ cause, so much so that the Eurovision Commission demanded the rainbow flag should not become an emblem of provocation.

Again, in 2013, Finland's Krista Siegfrids made a stand for legalising same-sex marriage. Costumed in a wedding dress, Krista taunted conservative Europe when she kissed her female backing dancer during her performance of *Marry Me*. And in 2014 the call for acceptance and gender fluidity was highlighted when a bearded Tom Neuwirth won Eurovision for Austria, performing as his stage persona Conchita Wurst. Once again, Eurovision led the way and Europe followed. Even the outrageous gimmick songs that have become both the lifeblood and the bane of Eurovision seem to come with subliminal political subtext.

The Eurovision trajectory of Ireland is worthy of analysis. Back in the 1960s, as a fledgeling republic, resources were tight. Consequently, Ireland seldom featured in international competition. For the most part Irish national pride was achieved in the reflected glory of the Irish diaspora. Then along came Eurovision. Instinctively, the Irish national passion for singing songs seemed to level the playing pitch. The Irish embraced Eurovision as an opportunity to express national identity on an international stage.

Ireland holds the record of seven Eurovision wins and is the only country to have won the title three times consecutively. Even Ireland's interval act from 1994, *Riverdance*, became a worldwide sensation, grossing box-office receipts and introducing traditional Irish dance as a global phenomenon. But then, in 2008, just as the booming Celtic Tiger economy roared loudest, the unexpected happened.

Dustin the Turkey, a glove puppet in a shopping trolley chanting *Irelande douze pointe!*, was selected to represent Ireland in Eurovision. Euro-analysts suggest it was an expression of Ireland's coming of age, an arrogance bred of the booming economy. This parody of parodies raised a feathered finger of superiority to the world. Some say it was genius, others say it was ghastly. Maybe it was Ireland's crude way of stepping out of the spotlight, making way for the new Eastern European republics to take centre stage. Regardless of the subliminal intention, Dustin the Turkey will be remembered as Ireland's Eurovision swansong.

The opening salvo of the most recent Russo-Ukrainian War ensured that Eurovision 2022 would not be without controversy. Alina Pash, the singer selected to represent Ukraine, was accused of illegally travelling to Russian-annexed Crimea, an allegation she vehemently denied. But to avoid what she described as a *virtual war and hatred*, Alina stepped down from the competition and was replaced by Kalush Orchestra.

Had it been any other year, Europundits and *músicos* all agree that the sensational Sam Ryder, with his showstopping performance of *Space Man*, would achieve victory for the UK. But European opinion consolidated behind a campaign to secure a massive and unprecedented public vote for Ukraine. And when the final scores were tallied, Kalush Orchestra had leapfrogged from a floundering fourth position to outright winners. The free and democratic voice of Europe stood shoulder to shoulder with Ukraine and had spoken as one.

Magnanimous in defeat, Sam Ryder's integrity shone through in the true spirit of Eurovision when he sent his love and support to the besieged people of Ukraine.

Due to the unabating conflict, Ukraine is unable to host this year's contest. Call it a Eurovision solution to a European problem, but it seemed right, fair and appropriate when the BBC stepped up to the mark. And so, for the first time since 1998, Eurovision is coming home to the UK.

At its core Eurovision is a pop-music extravaganza. Boom Bang-a-Bang and Jaja Ding Dong might raise a wry smile, but to dismiss it as trite would be an error of judgement. This is the soundtrack of Pax Europa.

Eurovision is lightning in a bottle – as elusive as Europe itself. Therein lies the secret of its success – that ability to renew, reinvent, react has made Eurovision a zeitgeist barometer that thrives on the lifeblood, soul and marrow of what it means to be European at any snapshot moment in time.

And I'm Thinking …

I know not with what weapons World War III will be fought,
but World War IV will be fought with sticks and stones.
Albert Einstein, *Liberal Judaism* (April–May 1949)

Even Albert Einstein, one of the greatest minds of the twentieth century, could not have anticipated that World War III would be fought with nothing more than a squirt of hand sanitiser and two verses of *Happy Birthday.*

By the dawn of the twenty-first century the anticipated rules of engagement for World War III had changed and changed utterly. The arrival of the pan-national, New Age eco-warrior movement informed us that the next Great Global Conflict would not be a nation-versus-nation old-style military exercise. World War III would not be a battle for territory, nor would it be a clash of opposing ideologies. No – the next war to end all wars would be ecological rather than ideological and would demand the banding together of the entire human race and human resources to fight against some greater, as yet unknown and unquantified, natural catastrophe of global proportion.

Two years ago the future of our planet came into sharp focus when a fifteen-year-old schoolgirl stepped out from behind the barricades. Her words cut through the racket of sabre-rattling and rhetoric, and world leaders sat up and took notice.

Greta Thunberg was that modern-day Joan of Arc; her message was global and simple. She reached out to every living soul across the seven continents.

— My message is the same to everyone, she said. — We must unite behind the science and act on the science.

Like the prophets of old, she insisted she was but a conduit to a greater knowledge, a greater power. And when our leaders reassured her, saying,

— I am listening to you, Greta …

… her rebuke was as sharp as it was blunt.

— Don't listen to me, she snapped. — Listen to the scientists.

Our leaders waffled and the war on climate change was once again long-fingered.

And though we all agreed that The End of the World is Nigh, we relaxed in the comfort of our First World lifestyle, sitting smugly at the top of the food chain, reassured by our self-proclaimed superior intellect. We were confident that *nigh* would not be coming anytime soon, and certainly not in our lifetime.

But then, just when we least expected it – World War III erupted with a full-force broadside when Covid-19 hit the planet. Our expert strategists all agreed: this is a pandemic. In the absence of a vaccine, there would be deaths, many deaths. An uncurtailed spike in infections would overrun our frontline medical defences and lead to an exponential rise in human mortality. The greatest scientists and medical minds on the planet assembled and devised a definitive battle plan.

Phase one of World War III was to be a rearguard action of damage limitation. We had to *flatten the curve*. This would give medical science some chance to limit the carnage of the first shock wave of attack. The strategy was clear: self-quarantine and social isolation. Non-combatants (Joe and Josephine Public) must stay in our homes, for the virus lurks within the non-combatant community. Movement of people would stop.

Our normal social discourse through work and play was to cease immediately. Shops, pubs, sporting and entertainment events would be shut down. The message was clear. Stay home and – *flatten the curve*. We were warned that if we continued recklessly unchecked, the net result would be to – *cull the herd*.

An interesting aspect of human group dynamics is our ability to react to any given situation with either *herd behaviour* or *pack instinct*.

In simple terms, *herd behaviour* is typified by skittish reaction – mass hysteria that leads to a stampede mentality – in comparison to *pack instinct*, which is a dynamic of cooperation working towards a common goal.

In times of crisis, humans function most efficiently when we rely on our pack instinct. We work best when restructured as small groups with strong, trusted leadership working towards a common goal for the greater good. In the face of this pandemic, under the guidance of good leadership, small groups would isolate from the herd and work as individual packs for the greater good. That was the plan, plain and simple.

But the initial denial, dithering and mixed messages by some of our most powerful and influential opinion leaders created uncertainty among the herd. The message they delivered was not simple, the plan was ever-changing, and the strategy was unclear. This confused our pack instinct and encouraged our herd reaction, leading to some bizarre behaviour – not least, the insane stockpiling of toilet paper in every home across the globe.

There were rumours of massive government budgets spent on PPE that was not fit for purpose, and whisperings of potential preferential distribution of vaccines if and when they were developed. But most worrying of all was the apocryphal tales circulating among the general public that strict government directives were being ignored and flaunted by government officials at the highest level – all very reminiscent of Orwell's:

– Four legs good, two legs better! All animals are equal.

But some animals are more equal than others.

And so, I sit here looking out on the deserted streets of my hometown. Life as we knew it has ground to a standstill, with not so much as a contrail in the sky. Day after day, spiralling infection rates continue to be broadcast to a terrified public and, night after night, iconic centres of global population are presented divested of human life. It's as if our world has degenerated into a science-fiction B-movie – a dystopian global scenario that would not be unfamiliar to Austin Powers. The whole world in lockdown.

And I'm thinking …

At a basic practical level, the Covid-19 crisis could be used as a social experiment that offers an opportunity to examine how we as a species will react to an imminent global crisis. The sceptic in me feels not much will be learnt from 2020. The cynic in me imagines a future of unchecked climate change – our leaders and those who should know better, with their trousers rolled up beyond their knees and they paddling around in the rising water levels at the foothills of Mount Everest – reciting the mantra,

– Fake News! Fake News!

But the eternal optimist in me believes that we will remember the words of Greta Thunberg when she insisted,

– We must unite behind the science and act on the science.

Nobody knows if or when World War III, this war against Covid-19, will end. I've heard some say it will all be over by Christmas. Where have we heard that before?

When all this is over, and we honour our dead and count the costs, let us look back on 2020 with 20/20 vision and learn something. Let us hope that when the next call to arms resounds around the world that neither party political expediency nor partisan national interests will take precedence over human survival.

And I'm thinking ...

Maybe Albert Einstein was correct when he predicted,

— World War IV will be fought with sticks and stones.

McKenzie's Gate, Pine Street.

Biography

Presented with: *The Leonardo da Vinci World Award of Arts 2024*
[The World Cultural Council, Switzerland].
The Irish Books, Arts & Music Award 2024
[American Irish Heritage Centre, Chicago].

Cónal Creedon is a novelist, playwright and documentary film maker.

His collection of short fiction, *Pancho and Lefty Ride Again* (2021) was awarded One City One Book 2022, and the Bronze Award Next Generation Book Awards USA 2022 (finalist). His novel, *Begotten Not Made* (2018), has achieved literary award recognition: the Eric Hoffer Award USA 2020, the Bronze Award Next Generation Book Awards USA 2020, Finalist in the Montaigne [Most Thought-Provoking Book] Award USA 2020, Nominated for the Dublin International Book Award 2020. Book of the Year Irish Examiner 2020. Top Books of the Year – Liveline RTÉ Irish National Radio. Other books by Cónal Creedon include, *Cornerstone* (2017), *The Immortal Deed of Michael O'Leary* (2015), *Second City Trilogy* (2007), *Passion Play* (1999) cited as Book of the Year BBC Radio 4, *Pancho And Lefty Ride Out* (1995).

Award-winning plays include; *The Trial of Jesus* (2000), which featured as part of the Irish National Millennium celebrations, received two Business to Arts Awards by President of Ireland, Mary McAleese and was nominated for an Irish Times Special Judges Theatre Award 2000. *Glory Be To The Father* (2001), produced by Red Kettle Theatre Company, Waterford. Cónal's *Second City Trilogy* of stage plays achieved high acclaim from theatre critics in Shanghai, New York and Ireland. *The Second City Trilogy* picked up several awards at the 1st Irish Theatre Awards New York, including Best Actor, Best Director and nominated Best Playwright. *When I Was God*, from the *Second City Trilogy* was also awarded Best Actor and Best Supporting Actor at ICA Federation Awards 2014. In 2021 it was awarded Best Production, Best Actor and Best Director at the Irish National Play Awards.

Cónal's film documentaries achieved high critical acclaim – shortlisted for the Focal International Documentary Awards UK and numerous broadcasts by RTÉ [Irish National Television] with international screenings at Féile an Phobail West Belfast Festival, World Expo Shanghai, China, Origin Theatre Festival New York, USA, the Irish National Centenary Commemorations and at NYU New York University, USA.

Cónal has written and produced more than 60 hours of original radio drama broadcast by RTÉ, BBC, CBC, ABC. Cited as Best Radio by Irish Times radio critics 1996 and 1998.

Recognition for
Contribution to the Arts

- Presented with The Leonardo da Vinci World Award of Arts 2024 [The World Cultural Council, Switzerland].
- Presented with The Irish Books, Arts & Music Award 2024 [American Irish Heritage Centre, Chicago].
- Cumann Iarscoláirí na Mainistreach Thuaidh. Person of The Year Award 2021
- Appointed (Covid-Pandemic) Goodwill Literary Ambassador for Cork City 2020
- Awarded Lord Mayor's Culture Award 2020
- Appointed Culture Ambassador for Cork City 2020
- Invited Guest of Honour, 10th Anniversary Shanghai Writers' China 2018
- Nominated Cork Person of the Year 2018
- Appointed Adjunct Professor of Creative Writing UCC 2017
- Appointed Heritage Ambassador for Cork City 2017
- Keynote Speaker Daniel Corkery Summer School, Inchigeela, Ireland 2016
- Keynote Speaker Merriman Summer School, Glór, Ennis, Ireland 2015
- Keynote Speaker Launch Cork Europa Erlesen, Irish Embassy Berlin, Germany 2014
- Invited Scholarship Forum, Fudan University, Shanghai, China 2008
- Invited Speaker 7-City Reading Tour, Irish American Cultural Institute, USA 2008
- Nominated Cork Person of the Year 2001
- Awarded Lord Mayor's Culture Award 1999

Theatre

2021	When I Was God – Special Covid Production – The Irish National Play Awards. Awarded Best Production, Best Actor and Best Director at Irish National Play Awards
2019	The Cure – Arlene's Grocery, New York
2016	The Cure – Irish Arts Centre Queens, New York
2014	When I Was God – Fletcher and Camross Drama. ICI Festival Awarded Best Actor. ICI Federation Drama Festival Awards Awarded Best Supporting Actor. ICI Federation Drama Awards
2013	The Cure – USA Premiere. Green Room Theatre New York Awarded Best Actor. 1st Irish Theatre Awards New York Nominated Best Playwright. 1st Irish Theatre Awards New York
2011	The Cure – JUE International Arts Festival, Shanghai. China
2011	The Cure – Halfmoon Theatre. Cork Opera House. Ireland
2010	When I Was God & After Luke Chinese Premiere, Shanghai World Expo
2010	When I Was God & After Luke – Cork Arts Theatre. Ireland
2009	When I Was God & After Luke – (Irish Rep Theatre New York) Awarded Best Director 1st Irish Theatre Awards New York Nominated Best Actor 1st Irish Theatre Awards New York Nominated Best Production 1st Irish Theatre Awards New York
2008	When I Was God – USA Premiere [Green Room New York)
2005	The Cure – Cork Opera House/ Blood in the Alley Theatre Co.
2005	After Luke – Cork Opera House/Blood in the Alley Theatre Co.
2005	The Second City Trilogy – Comm European Capital of Culture
2002	When I Was God – Madder Market, 3 Cities Festival, Norwich, UK
2001	Glory Be To The Father – Red Kettle Theatre Company National Tour: Waterford, Kilkenny, Cork, Galway, Sligo
2001	When I Was God – Everyman Palace Theatre, Cork, Ireland
2001	When I Was God – Bewley's Theatre, Dublin, Ireland
2000	The Trial Of Jesus – Corcadorca Theatre Company. Featured as part of the National Millennium Celebrations. Awarded two National Business to Arts Awards. Nominated for Irish Times Theatre Awards
1999	When I Was God – Red Kettle Theatre Company

Books

2021   *Pancho and Lefty Ride Again – a collection of short fiction published by Irishtown Press Ltd.*
– Awarded One City One Book 2022
– Finalist Next Generation Book Awards USA 2022

2018   *Begotten Not Made – a novel published by Irishtown Press Ltd.*
– Awarded the Eric Hoffer Award for commercial fiction 2020, USA
– Bronze Award in NGBA Book Awards 2019, USA
– Finalist the Montaigne Award 'Most Thought-Provoking Book' 2020, USA
– Listed for the Dublin International Book Award 2020 (to be announced)
– Shortlisted for Readers Favourite Book Awards 2018, USA.
– Cited as Best Book of the Year – Irish Examiner.
– Listed as Books to Read for 2020 – Liveline RTÉ.

2017   *Cornerstone – Editor of anthology of UCC student writing. Published by UCC & Cork City Libraries.*

2015   *Immortal Deed of Michael O'Leary – published by Cork City Libraries.*

2007   *Second City Trilogy – a trilogy of internationally award-winning stage plays, published by Irishtown Press Ltd. Commissioned by European Capital of Culture 2005. Productions in China, USA and Ireland.*
Awarded Best Director. 1st Irish Theatre Awards New York, 2009.
Nominated Best Production. 1st Irish Theatre Awards New York, 2009.
Awarded Best Actor. 1st Irish Theatre Awards New York, 2013.
Nominated Best Playwright. 1st Irish Theatre Awards New York, 2013.
Awarded Best Actor. ICI Federation Drama Festival Awards, 2014.
Awarded Best Supporting Actor. ICI Federation Drama Festival Awards, 2014.

1999	*Passion Play – a novel cited as,*
	– Book of the Year (BBC Radio 4)
	– Book of the Week (The Irish Examiner)
	– Book on One (RTÉ 1 – Irish National Radio)
	– Book of the Week (RAI – Italian National Radio)
	Translated into Italian and Bulgarian, with extracts published in Germany, China.
1995	*Pancho and Lefty Ride Out – a collection of short stories. published by The Collins Press. Short stories have been adapted for stage, film and radio.*
	Short stories have been published and broadcast extensively in news-papers, magazines, literary periodicals and collections.
	With translation into German, and China – Cónal's short fiction gained recognition in
	– Life Extra Short Story Awards
	– Francis Mac Manus Short Story Awards
	– George A. Birmingham Short Story Awards
	– One-Voice Monologue Awards BBC
	– The PJ O'Connor Awards.

Radio Drama

Cónal has penned over 60 hours of original fiction, short stories and plays for radio. His work represented Ireland in the World Play International Radio Drama Festival 2000 and was subsequently broadcast on participating networks: BBC Radio 4, ABC (Australia), RTHK (Hong Kong), LATW (USA), CBC (Canada), BBC World Service, RNZ (New Zealand), RTÉ.

2005	*Adventure of the Downtown Dirty Faces. (5 short stories – RTÉ Radio)*
2005	*No. 1, Devonshire Street (BBC Radio 4 & BBC World Service)*
2004	*Adaptation – Tailor and Ansty (RTÉ Drama)*
2004	*Passion Play – Book on One. (RTÉ Radio)*
2003	*The Prodigal Maneen (Awarded the C of I Bursary RTÉ)*
2003	*Adaptation – Guests of the Nation (Frank O' Connor Centenary – RTÉ)*
2002	*The Cure (Monologue – RTÉ)*
2001	*1601 The March of O'Sullivan Beara (Docu/drama Battle of Kinsale)*
2000	*This Old Man, He Played One (World Play International Fest.)*
1994-98	*Under the Goldie Fish (85 half-hour episodes – RTÉ)*
	Listed one of Best Radio Programmes in 1996 & 1998 – The Irish Times.
1994	*After the Ball (Francis MacManus Awards)*
1994	*Every Picture Tells a Story (RTÉ Radio 1)*
1994	*Caught in a Trap (C.L.R Drama Competition RTÉ)*
1993	*Come Out Now, Hacker Hanley! (RTÉ Radio)*

TV Documentary/Film

2010   *Flynnie, The Man Who Walked Like Shakespeare (Producer/writer/ director).*

          Nominated Focal Documentary Awards. London, UK.

2007   *The Boys Of Fairhill (Producer/writer/director) Screened RTÉ.*

2006   *If It's Spiced Beef (Producer/writer/director) Screened RTÉ.*

2006   *Why The Guns Remained Silent In Rebel Cork (Writer/director) Screened RTÉ.*

2005   *The Burning of Cork (Writer/director)*

          Screened RTE. Cork Archives. Cork City Hall & World Expo Shanghai 2010.

          NYU (New York University) USA, West Belfast Festival, Origin Theatre New York USA.

          Public screening as part of the official Irish Government Centenary Celebrations.

2001   *A Man of Few Words (Short film produced by Indie Films)*
          Screened on RTÉ & various film festivals.

1995   *The Changing Faces of Ireland. RTÉ (co-scripted six-part series)*
          Screened on RTÉ.

Recorded Collaborations

Collaborations include:

- Singer songwriter John Spillane
- Singer-songwriter Claire Sands
- Small Birds [Sound Artists: Irene Murphy, Mick O'Shea & Harry Moore] – One City One Book. 2022
- Orchestral composer, John O'Brien, and Cork Opera House Orchestra. 2021
- DJs Greg Dowling and Shane Johnson – Fish Go Deep, Magic Night by the Lee. 2021

Other

- Writer-in-Residence University College Cork. 2016
- Writer-in-Residence Shanghai Writers' Association. 2008
- Writer-in-Residence Cork Everyman Palace. 1999–2001
- Radio presenter for RTÉ & columnist with The Irish Times. 1999–2001
- Writer-in-Residence Cork County Council. 1998
- Writer-in-Residence Cork Prison. 1997

Special – Covid Online-Streaming Presentation/Productions

March 2022	*Knowledge: International institute of Influencers conference, IMS Law College Noida, India*
Feb 2022	*Creativity: Humanities, University of Rajasthan, Jaipur, India*
Dec 2021	*Present Artistic practice lecture IMS Law College Noida, India*
July 2021	*The Writer's Mindset – with Yvonne Reddin. Dublin Ireland*
June 2021 a.	*Cork City Hall, conference: Senior Chinese officials Program 2021, China*
June 2021 b.	*Cork City Hall, conference: Senior Chinese officials Program 2021, China*
May 2021	*LITREAL: The New Standard. Interviewed by Dr Shasikala Palsamy, India*
April 2021	*World Book Day, with Tina Pisco and Sara Baume. World Book Day*
March 2021	*St. Patrick's Day – The Traditions of St Patrick. The Crawford Gallery*
March 2021	*The Cure – Online streaming [Covid-19] Everyman Palace Theatre*
March 2021	*When I Was God – Online streaming – Everyman Palace Theatre*
March 2021	*After Luke – Online streaming – Everyman Palace Theatre*
Feb 2021	*Screening – Burning of Cork – 1st Irish Theatre Festival New York*
Feb 2021	*Yan Ge, Museum of Literature Ireland, Dublin. Chinese New Year*
Dec 2020	*Public Reading commemoration of Burning of Cork – Cork City Hall*
Dec 2020	*Screening of documentary – Burning of Cork – Cork City Hall*
Dec 2020	*Concert with John Spillane – Everyman Palace Theatre*
Nov 2020	*The Cure – Online streaming, Everyman Palace Theatre*
Nov 2020	*When I Was God – Online streaming, Everyman Palace Theatre*
Nov 2020	*After Luke – Online streaming, Everyman Palace Theatre*
Sept 2020	*Online film – Flavours of Cork – European Association – SPD – EU*
July 2020	*Filmed discussion: Story of portrait by Eileen Healy – Crawford Gallery Cork*
July 2020	*Féile an Phobail, documentary streamed and interview – Belfast*
June 2020	*Green Room – concert Cónal Creedon and John Spillane – Cork Opera House*

Reading Tours include

Switzerland	*James Joyce Foundation Zurich 2020.*
	Centre for Irish Studies Zurich University 2020.
Italy	*4 city Reading tour Italy – 2001.*
	Rome, Florence, Venice, Perugia.
UK	*Various reading tours.*
	Dylan Thomas Centre – Swansea. 2000.
	Filthy McNasty's – London. 2001.
	Madder Market Theatre – 3 Cities Festival – Norwich. 2002.
China	*Presented several reading tours to Shanghai, China.*
	Shanghai International Literary Festival. 2008.
	Fudan Uni. Shanghai, People's Uni. Shanghai, Le Chéile Shanghai.
	2009.
	Shanghai World Expo. 2010.
	Shanghai Jue International Arts Festival. 2010.
	M on the Bund & Shanghai Writer's Association. 2013.
	Guest of Honour – 10th Anniversary – Shanghai Writers' Association
	2017.
USA	*Irish American Cultural Institute, 7 city coast-to-coast reading tour*
	USA. 2007.
	New York, Albany, Rochester, Omaha, Montana, San Francisco, New
	Jersey.
	NYU – New York University 2019.
Austria	*Sprachsalz Literary Festival. Tyrol Austria. 2014.*
Berlin	*Launch of Cork Europa Erlesen – Translated by Jürgen Schneider.*
	2016.
	The Literaturwerkstatt Berlin festival 2011.
Ireland	*Numerous readings at literary festivals – Including,*
	Keynote Speaker at Daniel Corkery Summer School. 2019.
	Speaker at Merriman Summer School. 2014.

Selection of Reviews

Good writing knows no ethnicity. Good writing knows no nationality. Good writing is good writing – not alone is this good writing - It's excellent writing. Very personal writing. Very humorous writing. They say if Dublin was burnt down it could be rebuilt again by reading the work of James Joyce – well the very same could be said about Creedon's work – Cork city could be built from his words.

Malachy McCourt – WBAI RADIO New York.

The novel's interior is much indebted to Joyce. The way Creedon combines the child-centred perspective of *Paddy Clarke Ha! Ha! Ha!* with the tough teenage world of *The Commitments* and the domestic cruelty of *The Woman Who Walked into Doors* is ambitious and effective. His exposition of his characters' thought processes owes much to Flann O' Brien's skewed sophistication and Patrick McCabe's scabrous vision as to an earlier prototype of Seán O' Casey's Joxer. Creedon has found a form all of his own.

C.L. Dallat, Times Literary Review [TLS].

Fathers and sons and the damage done: this is the theme, with variations, of the Cork writer Cónal Creedon's fine plays *After Luke* and *When I Was God*, which can be seen in a nearly pitch-perfect production. Mr Creedon's words are enough to create a world that is at once comic and dramatic, poetic and musical.

Rachel Saltz, New York Times.

The highlight of last year's theatre in Shanghai came all the way from Cork in Irish playwright's Cónal Creedon's double-header of short plays – powerful, yet punctuated with humour, lyrical and richly colloquial. They were terrific!

That's Shanghai Magazine [China].

Irish playwrights (from Yeats and Wilde and Synge and Shaw on down to now) are always good going on great, and the latest in that endless chain is all but unknown in America, Cónal Creedon. Unknown no longer, Creedon's short, idiosyncratic *After Luke*, and even shorter, punchier *When I Was God*, comprise a disturbing two-hour double-bill. Idiosyncratic? Bite off any hunk of either work; it's all as chewy as leather yet weirdly digestible. None of this would be unfamiliar to, let's say, D. H. Lawrence, or, for that matter, George Orwell. What hasn't been heard before is the thorny voice of 48-year-old Cónal Creedon of County Cork, Ireland, who, from all reports, is a lot gentler in the flesh than on paper.

Jerry Tallmer, New York Villager.

They were discussing what should go into the Irish Millennium Time-Capsule. If they are looking for something to represent Ireland, how about Cónal Creedon's *Under the Goldie Fish*? It's so off the wall, that it shouldn't ring true, but the most frightening fact is that it does...

Eilís O'Hanlon, The Sunday Independent.

This is contemporary theatre that plays like the works of a past master. The work of Irish playwright Cónal Creedon, are quite simply a delight, [but] not in an all-sunshine and light way. On a sparse stage on which the characters can only live or die, it lives. Underlying all is a love of language and a keen observance of detail – Creedon is lyrical, and uses rhyme and rhythm, without being showy, and enriches with the Cork colloquial without alienating – Come back soon, you are always welcome on the Shanghai stage.

Talk Shanghai. China. Arts Editor.

As written by Cónal Creedon, such moments resound with wince-inducing authenticity before they are eclipsed by an inspirational twist – words, inflected with the faintly Scandinavian accent of Munster, soar like a bracing breeze off the River Lee.

Andy Webster, New York Times.

Under the Goldie Fish would make Gabriel García Márquez turn puce in a pique of jealousy... Gold card radio with plums on.

Tom Widger, The Sunday Tribune.

I don't know why Cónal Creedon hasn't been produced on Broadway yet. Certainly, his plays are as deserving as any recent work from Ireland that has made that cut. In fact, he has more to say, more concisely, than just about any of his dramatic contemporaries.

Cahir O'Doherty, Irish Central New York.

Vigorously sustained by stylish performances and an ingenious script, which marries comedy and pathos with a sure hand. They'll love it. It's impossible not to.

The Irish Times.

Everyone loves the Irish. It's just a fact. Creedon's script is a rich fusion of melancholy poetry and affable banter. Aidan O'Hare and *The Cure* are a match made in monologue heaven. Its potency lies in the profound ability of the playwright and the actor to connect directly with people. *The Cure* is a truly fine piece of theatre, one that is Irish to its core but anything but provincial in its scope. You couldn't ask for anything more than this.

Smart Shanghai Magazine.

Cónal Creedon's *Second City Trilogy* is a significant dramatic achievement. Creedon constructs predicaments for his characters that ring true universally. In three companion pieces that play logically together, the playwright puts a marginal view of society centre-stage, and, with warmth and humour, offers a view of life from the side lines. What ensues is a solid replaying of a classic and timeless family conflict. Taken altogether, the *Second City Trilogy* is an important a landmark in drama, its achievement is to find a theatrical language that can accommodate the poor and depressed Ireland that we have come from, and the new, confusing, complex reality we now find ourselves in. Creedon, director Geoff Gould, and the cast deserve credit not only for offering up an entertaining night of theatre, but for contributing to our understanding of where we have come from and where we are going. Any drama that can do both is indeed worthy of praise.

The Irish Examiner.

It's one of those books where it often feels inappropriate to either laugh or cry, at times surreal, frequently hilarious, often poignant but never, ever dull – The reader enters the twilight zone.

U Magazine.

Creedon can create characters, not just mouthing amusing philosophical meanderings, not just cold abstractions, these are creations of Creedon's great humanity. It is essential that I tell you here that you must finish this book. A wonderful inventive comedy.

The Sunday Tribune.

Creedon's rootedness in Cork qualifies him to chronicle the transformations that not just Cork City, but all of Ireland, caused by the economic boom of the 1990s – called the Celtic Tiger – and the aftermath. At times it feels Beckett-like, you might think the people are too unusual to exist, but they actually do.

New York City Arts.

I imagine there are few things harder to be than a contemporary Irish playwright. Given the theatrical history of the Emerald Isle, its lyric tradition, it must be either a very daring or very foolish individual indeed who steps up to be measured against the likes of the Irish literary pantheon. On the daring end falls Cónal Creedon, author of *After Luke* and *When I Was God*. The two plays are the latter parts of Creedon's serio-comic *Second City Trilogy*, focusing on life in present-day County Cork. Both plays are about the family dynamic, specifically the relationships between fathers and sons. In *After Luke*, two half-brothers, Maneen and Son, share a memory so terrible that it sets them at odds with each other all their lives. In the centre is Dadda, Maneen's father, who does his best to keep the peace but can only do so much. As he sagely says "…when two elephants go to war, 'tis the grass gets trampled."

In *When I Was God*, Dino lives in the shadow of his father's regrets, and under the pressure of his expectations. It's a classic plot, the father using the son to live the life he wished he could have had. To tell the rest would rob the reader of one of the funniest moments of the evening. Creedon's main device in these pieces is repetition. I found myself laughing uproariously as the words stayed the same, but the meaning was in constant shift, each repetition raising the stakes to a beautifully bittersweet conclusion – driving the action and the comedy. Creedon's show holds up very well against the pantheon of Irish theatre, taking chances with some very risky devices. It's a fun night out, and I'd be interested to see the trilogy in its entirety; if the first act is as entertaining as the last two, it would be well worth it.

Peter Schuyler, NY Theatre Review.

The Cure is a dramatic creation that straddles what we once were and what we have become. It examines closely the fracture at the heart of our contemporary experience – scavenging the thesaurus for sufficient superlatives for this fine piece of writing – yes, we liked it. We liked it a lot.

The Irish Examiner.

A one-man show at the Ke Center proves that you don't need a huge cast to produce a hit – their recent collaboration with Irishtown Productions proves that they are on top of their game. Cork playwright Cónal Creedon's gritty soliloquy *The Cure* saw Irish actor Aidan O'Hare command the stage as a man left behind by a racing economy and changing city. Creedon's use of language is dizzyingly attractive. He manipulates repetition to great effect, bringing the opening lines back several times in chilling sonata form. As for the staging, the Ke Center's stark space was the perfect backdrop for a bleak but redemptive piece of drama.

Asia City Network, Shanghai, China.

A pair of tenderly drawn plays by Cónal Creedon, set in Creedon's native Cork, probe the tough love and tough hurt – exchanged by men in Irish Families. Both plays – are intimately conceived and performed, tracing in chiaroscuro, the intersection between kinship and machismo.

New Yorker Magazine.

The Cure is the bittersweet tale of a man who has emotionally lost his way. As with the previous two plays, Creedon explores the frustrations of average lives, to the backdrop of historical happenings in the playwright's hometown. And as with the previous two, the script is lyrical and rich with colloquialism, the melancholy lifted with moments of delightful amusement. ("When the chemistry goes in a relationship, he reflects on marriage and drink, "There's nothing for it but to take more chemicals) – A fine piece of theatre …

That's Shanghai Magazine, Urbanatomy Shanghai.

A complex enthralling piece of theatre that boasts the dual achievement of entertaining and educating – a testament to Creedon's shrewd writing skill.

The Irish Independent.

I got to see *The Cure* at the Half Moon Theatre last night. It is terrific. It's great fun. It's just fantastic. Just so well done by Mikel Murfi. It's a credit to Cónal Creedon. Don't miss this play, you need to go and see it – the cultural highlight of Cork 2005.

Opinion Line 96fm.

Creedon's great gift seems to be observation, 45 tense, funny and pointed minutes, convincing and memorably skilful. *When I Was God*, is both a treat and a treasure.
The Irish Times.

This play operated on two levels; it was hilarious but poignant. Creedon's gift is his ability to distil the very essence of his environment. It is this sense of place and people and his gently anarchic view of life which makes his works so deliciously attractive.
The Irish Examiner.

Creedon's play shifts easily between the past and the present, revealing a sharp ear for dialogue, keen eye for observation and a deep affection for his characters as Creedon brings a deft pathos and humour to the tragicomedy of a peculiar father son relationship, a delight that demands to be savoured.
The Sunday Tribune.

BOOK OF YEAR – Highlights of the Year.
Cónal Creedon's recently published novel *Begotten Not Made* is a beguiling tale of tragic Christian Brother who forsook a potential love affair for the cloth having met a young nun on the night Dana won the Eurovision Song Contest.
Collette Sheridan – Highlights of the Year – Irish Examiner.

Selection of – BEST BOOKS OF THE YEAR.
It's a delight to read Cónal Creedon's *Begotten Not Made*. One of the most peculiar books I have read this year.
Theo Dorgan, Liveline. RTÉ Radio 1.

READERS' FAVORITE BOOK AWARDS USA.
★ ★ ★ ★ ★ This is a work of quirky and conceptual literary fiction. For readers who enjoy fully realized, unusual lead characters, look no further – Cónal Creedon has created what feels like a real person, on whose shoulders we sit as the narration takes us deep into his life and work, his philosophy, and his sense of love in moments which are both moving, bizarre and very amusing at times. The harsh backdrop of Irish life clashes beautifully with concepts of heavenly and mortal love, miracles, and strange appearances, painting a world which is ethereal in its fairy tale moments yet painfully recognizable and relatable too. I particularly enjoyed the dynamic dialogue,

as its pacing really moves scenes along. Overall, *Begotten Not Made* is a highly recommended read for literary fiction fans searching for truly unusual books that keep you thinking long after the last page is turned.

KC Flynn, Readers' Favourite Book Awards.

US REVIEW OF BOOKS.

This book spins a delicious yarn that tips nearly every sacred cow of Christianity– a timely sport in this era of diminished participation in monastic life and the laity's scathing criticism of the Church's sins and shortcomings – all the while spotlighting the archetypal unrequited romance made fresh in the monastic setting. In the backdrop is the soul of devout Irish Catholic culture and the lives of the working-class men and women of Cork who lend a down-to-earth stability to the tale as well as zest and colour. As a bonus, the author includes his fanciful pen-and-ink drawings and tasty stories within the story, such as Sister Claire's retelling of a saga about Mossie the Gardener and his war hero pigeon, Dowcha-boy. This is a plot thread sure to tickle even the most obstinate funny bone, and it specifically lends a magical yet realistic aura to what could have been a far more level, self-conscious story.

Creedon's well-honed, multidimensional cast of characters, his vividly portrayed settings and interiors of 1970s and contemporary Cork, and his measured but lyrical prose nail every nuance of the story arc. The author has ripped open his Irish heart to spill this marvellous pastiche, a real-life creed that must be absorbed with one's heart open wide to the pathos and poignancy of love lost and found, life lived and unlived, and spirituality bound to blind faith or soaring on the wings of perception. Ultimately, Creedon's tour de force pays tribute to an end-of-life journey that paradoxically celebrates the winter of regret and the eye-opening gift of having nothing left to lose.

Kate Robinson, US Review of Books.

I thoroughly enjoyed reading *Begotten Not Made* by Cónal Creedon – it maintains a Joycean flavour throughout the story. The writer's perspective in introducing the reverend brother's intellectual interpretation of authentic Biblical facts is so brilliant that it encourages you to fact check.

Ronald Clifford, Irish American Examiner. New York.

Cónal Creedon's new novel puts a magic-realist twist on the tale of a cleric's unrequited love for a nun. Brother Scully delves back through his analysis of scripture, which has led him to a unique and highly plausible theory regarding the true paternity of Jesus Christ. Inside the covers of *Begotten Not Made*, there unfolds a tale that's part poignant love story and part meditation on the phenomenon of faith, a uniquely Corkonian take on magical realism served up with Creedon's customary flair for colourful dialogue and tall tales – a fairy tale for the 21st Century.

Ellie O'Byrne, ARTS, Irish Examiner.

Begotten Not Made is rewarding, straddling a fine line between pathos and comedy. We see the disintegration of Brother Scully – between the torment of his unrealised love and his unique take on Catholicism, he doesn't believe in the divinity of Jesus and has a theory as to his real paternity. This is a troubled man, literally crumbling into a despairing heap as an elderly man. Brother Scully elicits sympathy despite his obnoxiousness – a hard man to like but Creedon's talent is to draw out the humanity of this demented individual. There is a lot more to this novel than sexual and spiritual frustration – It is funny, and it has real charm. There are elements of magic realism here which give the novel an air of fairy-tale. *Begotten Not Made* is well written, strong on highly amusing dialogue and has a twist that is satisfying, well worth the wait. Like all good art, the local becomes universal with its truths and its understanding of human nature.

Colette Sheridan, Weekend.

Last night I finished Cónal Creedon's *Begotten Not Made*. It is multi-layered, funny and touching, at times madcap or magic realist, quintessential storytelling, and has a wonderful and satisfying ending. It's about the unrequited love between Brother Scully and Sister Claire, a novitiate in the convent across the valley from his monastery in Cork city. That spiritual affair began on the night in 1970 that Dana won the Eurovision Song Contest, and it lasts for almost fifty years – their correspondence continues: Scully and Claire send a signal to each other every morning at dawn by quickly switching their bedroom light off and on. That one single act of devotion gives Scully the courage to live out his chaste life. But not all is how it seems. And there is a sting in this tail.

There are several poignant moments in the novel, the most moving of which is when towards the end of their hour or two together in 1970, in the garden, Scully and Claire are faced with a crucial decision. And that predicament, upon which their fates turned, reminded me of that great Cavafy poem, *Che fece... il gran rifiuto* (The Great Refusal)

Cónal has drawn a number of fine pen and ink illustrations to accompany the story which lends a charmingly quaint feeling to the rich reading experience.

Danny Morrison, Director of West Belfast Festival Féile an Phobail.

Begotten Not Made, a multi-faceted fairy-tale which gives a fresh twist to an ancient story – the life of Jesus. The book deftly presents an insight into human frailty: through the complicated love that arose between Br. Scully and Sr. Claire on the night Dana won the Eurovision. Equal parts hilarious and poignant. The story unfolds as Br. Scully grapples with his existence and his sanity and his unique exploration of the nature of belief. The book is also resplendent with illustrations by the author.

Aisling Meath, The Southern Star.

It's all there in *Begotten Not Made*, alongside the mysteries of the scripture, the alchemy of love, the pathos of life and the legend of a war hero racing pigeon: a picaresque epic that at times dips into the surreal.

Donal O'Donoghue, Books. RTÉ Guide.

Begotten Not Made is incredibly nuanced in that sympathy. Brother Scully is developed far beyond the definitions of his profession, beyond the collar, he is intellectual, emotional, sensitive and troubled. Such nuance is explored intricately in Cónal's classic, conversational style, ranging from profound humour to tinges of sadness and airs of dark comedy. The humour of the novel is colourful in every sense of the word, which Cónal infuses to dramatize the life of Brother Scully's adolescence. These playful anecdotes are threaded throughout the novel giving the lives of the characters depth and sincerity. At the end, the book is really set in that one hour, a feature reminiscent of Joyce.

Liz Hession, Motley Magazine.

What a rollicking good read it is. I have to confess that the Dowcha Boy pigeon business remained my favourite since it is so hilarious. But there were many such laugh out loud moments to be met with exclamation points in the margins. That whole Eurovision conceit was just brilliant. And coming round again and again to the flashing of the dawn lights. Loved the surreal moment when Scully walks off on the beam of light. And the great switcheroo of the ending was terrific. Wonderfully enjoyable book. Thanks a mill', Cónal!

David Monagan, Jaywalking With the Irish.

If there has been a sense that some documentaries on the Hidden Histories series have struggled to fully fill out the one-hour slot available, this was not the case with *Hidden History: The Burning of Cork* (RTÉ 1, Tuesday, 10:15pm). Instead, there was a sense that Neil Jordan (or indeed its own superb director, Cónal Creedon) could fruitfully be let loose on the story with a twenty-million-dollar budget. Creedon's documentary told far more than just the story of the night of December 11, 1920.

Village Magazine Dublin.

The Boys of Fairhill, Cónal Creedon's documentary which detailed the many accomplishments of 'the boys' in hurling, bowling, and dog-racing and pigeon fancying, indeed all the recreations which make a man's life worth living. The previous week Creedon had another erudite and evocative documentary about Cork, *If It's Spiced Beef*…and RTÉ is lucky to have him."

The Sunday Independent.

The impossibly surreal, hilarious, and often poignant series, *Under the Goldie Fish*

Evening Herald.

For distinctive flavour, free rein to the imagination and even the odd passionate belief, there may never be a match for *Under the Goldie Fish*…Cónal Creedon's mad, bad, wonderful-to-know daily sitcom-soap… If you like your metafictions, intertextuality and just plain messin' in daily doses – Creedon's yer only man!"

The Irish Times.

Reviews of Readings by
Cónal Creedon

Don't be fretting now about the past gone glories of Irish literary genius since we're lucky to have walking among us Cónal Creedon whom I not only had the personal pleasure of meeting as fellow author in the Sprachsalz festival [Austria] but heard the man read his work. The brilliance was self-evident and undeniable. The audience were in raptures over the beauty of his sentences and rapier-like wit. He writes about the human condition in ways that find you deep down where you just have to laugh and weep. Read this author and your faith will be restored in both literature and life.

Alan Kaufmann. – [Author of: Jew Boy, American Outlaw Book of Poetry]. Sprachsalz Festival Austria, 2016

The members of the Merriman Summer School were utterly enthralled by Cónal Creedon's presentation of a selection of his writings – a presentation that was warm, deeply insightful, and so humorous and entertaining about the human condition. He was by far one of the most able speakers at the school.

William J Smyth, Emeritus Professor UCC. Merriman Summer School, 2015

Cónal Creedon gave a tour de force reading of his work as it applies to the theme of 'love and marriage' at the 2015 Merriman Summer School in Ennis, Co. Clare. The audience reacted to Cónal's brilliant writing.

Professor Linda Connolly, Director Merriman Summer School, 2015

Cónal Creedon's presentation to Rochester in 2008 is still being spoken about. He established an easy and lasting rapport with the audience in his talk, Cork, the Center of the Universe as he shared slides that proved his point with humour and intelligence. It would be grand to have a return visit from this literary giant!

Elizabeth Osta – President of the Irish American Cultural Institute. (IACI) 7-city USA coast-to coast IACI Reading Tour

Cónal Creedon was a massive hit, a festival highlight and I hope he will come back.

Pat McCabe – Flat Lake Festival, 2011

Cónal Creedon brought the house down at this year's Flat Lake Festival, any comic would envy the laughs he elicited from the audience.

Eoin Butler-Kennedy – The Irish Times – July 2011.

A Humorous Reading Creedon reads from his work … Creedon is a skilful reader, managing to keep the crowd engaged, a challenging feat for many writers who are often able to captivate with the written word and less with the spoken. Creedon is able to capture the simple moments of people's lives with honesty and humour.

The crowd finds his work quite humorous as he speaks of "battling the beast" (a pig) and anecdotes of St. Patrick, Protestantism, Catholicism, Freemasons, and other topics worthy of a laugh when written of skilfully. The passage relates the tale of the life, death, and funeral of the character's father. "It's a strange thing to carry your father in a box," he reads as detailing the humorous ordeal of trying to carry the father to the funeral in a coffin he himself handcrafted.

Shanghai International Literary Festival. Shanghai City Weekend – Trista Marie [Lit Review THAT'S Shanghai].

A mention, too, to Cónal Creedon. He is the A No. 1 writer of Cork, in my estimation, and absolutely should be known more broadly internationally; he has the ear for every corner conversation, every magnificent touch of endearing absurdity he encounters. He's known well enough in Ireland but should have longer stilts by far. Find him, try him. He went on for a half hour about his father's years' long construction of his own coffin and had every single mug laughing in stitches – about his father's intricately planned demise. Chalk this whole experience down to the category What I Love Best About Ireland. I mean – that you can dream about a man you never met

David Monaghan – Ireland Unhinged & Jaywalking With the Irish.

The Spring Literary festival [2010] was incredibly successful this year. Aside from the quality of the writers and some of the amazing performances (Cónal Creedon and Martin Espada especially wowed) audience figures were consistently large at each event. We were obliged to move to a bigger venue for the fourth day to avoid breaking fire regulations on overcrowding.

Pat Cotter – Artistic Director Munster Literature Centre, Éigse Literary festival 2010.

Cónal Creedon at the Rock on The Fall's Road – stole the show and the hearts of everyone who heard him that afternoon. A highlight of the West Belfast Féile.

Danny Morrison, Director of West Belfast Festival Féile an Phobail.

Printed in Great Britain
by Amazon

8e8ed5ec-e53a-4381-a2c5-fa31849358ddR01